WORLD WAR 2
STORIES FOR KIDS

UNFORGETTABLE STORIES OF COURAGE, COMPASSION, AND HEROISM
INSPIRING TALES OF PATRIOTISM AND BRAVERY

YOUNG HEROES OF HISTORY SERIES

CONTENTS

Introduction 7

Chapter 1: What Started World War II? 11
    1.1 The Rising Tensions 11
    1.2 The War Begins 13
    1.3 The Role of Allies and Axis 15
    1.4 The Global Impact 17

Chapter 2: The Skies of War - Battles Above and Beyond 21
    2.1 The Battle of Britain: Sky Wars 21
    2.2 The Pearl Harbor Attack: A Day of Infamy 23
    2.3 The D-Day Invasion: Turning the Tide 25
    2.4 The Battle of the Bulge: A Surprise Attack 27

Chapter 3: Life on the Homefront -
The Hidden Heroes of War 31
    3.1 Life in a World at War 31
    3.2 Rationing and Victory Gardens 33
    3.3 The Role of Women and Children 35
    3.4 Stories of Hope and Resilience 37

Chapter 4: Unlikely Heroes: Ordinary People in Extraordinary Times 41
    4.1 The Story of Audie Murphy: From Farm Boy to Hero 41
    4.2 The Navajo Code Talkers: Secret Messengers 43
    4.3 The Tuskegee Airmen: Breaking Barriers............................. 45
    4.4 The Story of Nancy Wake: The White Mouse 46

Chapter 5: Unheard Voices and Unseen Heroes 51
    5.1 The Story of Irena Sendler: Life in a Jar................................ 51
    5.2 The Story of Chiune Sugihara: The Japanese Schindler 53
    5.3 The Story of the White Rose: Voices of Resistance 55
    5.4 The Story of Noor Inayat Khan: The Spy Princess 57

Chapter 6: The Furry and Feathered Heroes of World War II ... 61
    6.1 The Story of G.I. Joe: The Pigeon That Saved Lives............... 61
    6.2 The Story of Chips: The Dog Who Fought a War 63
    6.3 The Story of Antis: The Brave Dog in the Skies...................... 64
    6.4 The Story of Judy: The Dog that Became a Prisoner of War .. 66

Chapter 7: The Dawn After Darkness: The End of World War II and the Birth of a New Era............ 71
    7.1 Victory in Europe (VE) Day: The End of Fighting in Europe. 71
    7.2 Victory over Japan (VJ) Day: The End of World War II 73
    7.3 The Nuremberg Trials: A Fight for Justice............................. 75
    7.4 The Formation of the United Nations: A Hope for Peace 77

Chapter 8: Echoes of the Past: The Importance of Remembering World War II 81
    8.1 The Importance of Remembrance 81

8.2 World War II Memorials Around the World 83

8.3 How World War II is Commemorated 85

8.4 Continuing the Legacy: The Role of Stories 87

Chapter 9: Lessons of Valor: Unraveling the Teachings of World War II 91

9.1 Learning from the Past: The Importance of History 91

9.2 The Power of Unity and Cooperation 93

9.3 Understanding the Value of Peace 95

9.4 The Role of Individuals in Shaping History 97

Conclusion 101

References 103

"We know that enduring peace cannot be bought at the cost of other people's freedom."

- Franklin D. Roosevelt, January 1941

INTRODUCTION

Alright, you eager young history buffs, I see that gleam in your eyes! You're ready to dive helmet-first into the stirring tales of World War II, aren't you? Buckle up because we're about to zip back in time like a spitfire zooming through the sky. But fear not, we won't be showing you the grisly stuff. It's going to be an age-appropriate adventure, I promise. We'll focus on the bravery, courage, and oh-so-inspiring acts of heroism!

Now, World War II...What a time that was! Nations across the globe were locked in a conflict that was as massive as an elephant and as complicated as a Rubik's cube. But don't worry; we're not here to dump a heap of boring dates and dreary details on your plate.

Instead, we're going to meet some extraordinary young heroes – the kind of folks who remind us that sometimes, age is just a number. They were just like you, young and full of life, but boy, did they step up when the world needed them! Their stories of courage and compassion are like hot chocolate for the soul – warm, comforting, and oh-so-delicious!

But why, you may wonder, are we taking this trip down memory lane? Well, my young friend, it's not just about learning what happened. It's about understanding why it happened and how it changed our world. It's about seeing these young heroes in action and thinking, "Hey, I can be brave like that, too!" We're not just here to read history but to learn from it!

So, are you ready to zoom back in time and meet these young heroes? Excellent! Grab your helmet, hold on tight, buckle up, and go on a journey of courage, compassion, and heroism!

Remember, these stories are much like a rollercoaster ride. They'll lift you high, drop you low, twist you around, and leave your heart pounding. But don't worry, you're in safe hands! As an author, a history enthusiast, and your companion on this journey, I'll make sure the ride is as smooth as thrilling. So, let's dive in, shall we?

"As long as there are sovereign nations possessing great power, war is inevitable."

– Albert Einstein, November 1945

CHAPTER 1:
What Started World War II?

Ever tried to untangle a knot? One that's so twisted and tangled you can't figure out where it begins? Well, that's a bit like trying to understand the origins of World War II. It's a complex knot of events, decisions, and circumstances. But don't fret! We're going to untangle this together, thread by thread. So, let's start with the first few threads: the rising tensions before the war.

1.1 The Rising Tensions
The Great Depression and its Global Effects
It all started in the 1930s when the world was caught in the icy grip of the Great Depression. Much like when you're sick and can't play outside, the world's economies are down, and you can't play the money-making game. The stock market crash in 1929 sent shockwaves around the globe. Jobs were lost, businesses were shuttered, and people were left destitute. It was like a game of musical chairs; only when the music stopped did no chairs leave.

In Germany, the Depression hit particularly hard. The country was already struggling to pay off its debts from World War I. With the Depression, it was like trying to climb a mountain with a giant backpack. It was tough and exhausting.

Rise of Dictators: Hitler in Germany, Mussolini in Italy

In such troubled times, people often look for someone to blame and someone to follow, someone who promises a better future. Enter the dictators.

In Germany, Adolf Hitler and his Nazi Party rose to power. Hitler was like a school bully, blaming others for his problems. He pointed fingers at the Jews, Communists, and others, blaming them for Germany's woes. He promised to restore Germany's glory, and many people who were desperate for change believed him.

Meanwhile, in Italy, Benito Mussolini and his Fascist Party had already been in power since the 1920s. Mussolini was like that big kid on the playground who wanted all the toys for himself. He dreamed of building a new Roman Empire and started flexing Italy's muscles on the world stage.

Aggression of Japan in Asia

Halfway across the world in Asia, another country was stirring up trouble. Under Emperor Hirohito's rule, Japan was hungry for power and resources. Imagine being at a birthday party and seeing a huge cake on the table. You want a slice, but you also want the cherries, the icing, the whole thing! That's how Japan felt about Asia. It had already taken control of Korea and parts of China and was eyeing the rest of East Asia and the Pacific.

These rising tensions were a thread in the knot that would become World War II. The world watched as Germany, Italy, and Japan flexed their muscles, but it was like watching a storm brewing on the horizon. Everyone hoped it would blow over, but instead, it was about to blow up into the most devastating war in human history.

So, as we navigate these choppy historical waters together, remember this: History isn't just about dates and facts. It's about people, decisions, and events. It's about understanding why things happened the way they did and learning from them. And as we untangle this knot, you'll see that even in the darkest times, there are stories of courage, resilience, and hope. Stories that remind us of the extraordinary things ordinary people can do. Stories that show us the power of unity, compassion, and bravery. Stories that inspire us to be the best we can be.

But before we delve further into these inspiring tales, let's continue our exploration of the events leading up to World War II. Because, as the saying goes, "those who do not learn history are doomed to repeat it." And trust me, World War II is not something we want to repeat.

So, are you ready to continue our adventure through time? Great! Let's press on and learn more about this monumental historical period's major events, key figures, and significant impacts. Next stop: The start of the war!

1.2 The War Begins

Alright, let's get back to our story. It's now 1939, the storm clouds have gathered, and the first flash of lightning strikes with Germany's invasion of Poland.

Invasion of Poland by Germany

Contemplate you're playing a game of chess. It's your move, and you decide to shake things up. That's pretty much what Germany did, but this was no game. On September 1, 1939, German troops marched into Poland. It was like a scene from a movie, with tanks rolling in and aircraft flying overhead, but this was real life, and the stakes were incredibly high.

Poland, you see, was sandwiched between Germany and the Soviet Union. And neither of these powerful neighbors was particularly friendly. The Polish army fought bravely, but Germany's strong military outmatched them.

Declaration of War by Britain and France
People in Britain and France watched these events unfold with a growing sense of unease. It was like seeing a friend getting picked on and realizing you had to step in. On September 3, 1939, that's exactly what they did. Britain and France declared war on Germany. It was a bold move, like standing up to a bully in the playground, and it marked the start of their active involvement in World War II.

Blitzkrieg: The Lightning War Strategy
Now, let's talk about Blitzkrieg, a word you might have heard before. It's a German term that means "lightning war," and it was a military strategy used by the Germans during World War II. See yourself in a lightning storm. It's fast, powerful, and leaves little time to react. That's Blitzkrieg in a nutshell.

German forces would strike quickly and intensely, concentrating their forces on a small area to break through enemy lines before the enemies had time to respond. Envision it like a swift karate chop to break a wooden board. Once the line was broken, the German forces spread out rapidly, encircling and confusing their enemies. It was like spinning your little brother around until he's so dizzy he can't stand up straight.

This highly effective strategy led to Germany's quick conquest of Poland. Though brave and determined, the Polish army could not withstand the speed and force of the Blitzkrieg.

And so, World War II began. It was a time of uncertainty, anxiety, and fear. But it was also a time of courage, resilience, and unity. As we dive deeper into the nuances of this monumental event, remember that every decision, every battle, every victory, or loss is a part of the larger story of World War II. And within this vast story are countless tales of ordinary individuals performing extraordinary acts of bravery. We'll explore these tales while navigating World War II's stormy seas.

1.3 The Role of Allies and Axis

Let's visualize a schoolyard. Consider this scenario: two groups of kids, one on each end, ready for a game of tug-of-war. On one side, you've got the Allies: Britain, France, the Soviet Union, and eventually, the United States. On the other side, you have the Axis: Germany, Italy, and Japan. They're both pulling on their end of the rope, hoping to drag the other across the line in the middle. That's what the world looked like during World War II.

Formation of the Allies: Britain, France, Soviet Union, United States

The first ones to take a stand were Britain and France. They were like the two friends who always stood up for each other, even when things got tough. When Germany invaded Poland, they were quick to react. They declared war on Germany, standing firm like a solid wall against German aggression.

Eventually, they were joined by the Soviet Union and the United States. The Soviet Union, under the leadership of Joseph Stalin, joined the Allies in 1941. It was a bit like the school's star athlete joining your team. With the Soviet Union on their side, the Allies had a strong player to counter the Axis powers.

The United States, under President Franklin D. Roosevelt, joined the Allies in December 1941. It was after Japan attacked the U.S. naval base at Pearl Harbor. Project you're minding your own business, and suddenly, someone throws a snowball at you. That's how the United States felt. They declared war on Japan and, by extension, on the Axis powers.

Formation of the Axis: Germany, Italy, Japan

On the other side of the tug-of-war, we have the Axis powers. Under Adolf Hitler, Germany was the first to pull on the rope. Hitler was like that kid in school who always wanted his way, no matter what. He had big plans for Germany and was willing to go to great lengths to achieve them.

Italy, under Benito Mussolini, was quick to join Germany. Mussolini was like that kid who always hung out with the school bully, hoping to share power and glory. He dreamed of building a new Roman Empire and was ready to fight for it.

Japan, under Emperor Hirohito, joined the Axis in 1940. They were like that quiet kid in class who suddenly decided to join the school play. With resources running low in their country, they saw the war as a chance to secure the needed resources.

Key Leaders of Allies and Axis

Now, you might be wondering, who were the people calling the shots for these countries? Let's take a closer look.

For the Allies, we have Winston Churchill of Britain, Charles de Gaulle of France, Joseph Stalin of the Soviet Union, and Franklin D. Roosevelt of the United States. These leaders played a crucial role in guiding their countries through the war. They were like the team captains, making the tough decisions and cheering their teams on.

On the Axis side, we have Adolf Hitler of Germany, Benito Mussolini of Italy, and Emperor Hirohito of Japan. These leaders were the driving force behind the Axis powers. They were like the opposing team's coaches, devising strategies and pushing their teams to fight harder.

As we dig deeper into the stories of World War II, we'll meet these leaders and many more. We'll learn about their decisions, their actions, and the impact they had on the world. We'll see how ordinary people rose to the challenges of their time and became heroes in their own right.

And as we explore these stories, remember this: history is not just about the past. It's about understanding our world and our place in it. It's about learning from the past to create a better future. So, keep your eyes open, your mind curious, and your heart brave. There's a lot more to discover, a lot more to learn, and a lot more to inspire us.

1.4 The Global Impact

Picture this: you're playing with a water hose on a hot summer day in your backyard. You turn it on, and water sprays out, reaching your grass, the bushes, the flowers, and even the pesky weeds in the corners. That's just like World War II. It started in Europe and Asia, but its effects sprayed across the globe, touching every continent.

Spread of War to Africa and Asia

Let's think of the globe as a giant soccer ball. Each continent is like a different patch on the ball. Europe and Asia were the first patches to get caught up in the war. But soon, the conflict spread to Africa and further into Asia.

The North African Campaign was a tug-of-war between the Allies and Axis powers in Africa. It was like a seesaw, tilting this way and that as each side gained or lost ground. The Suez Canal and the Middle East oil fields were the coveted prizes. Ponder the idea that these are the last slices of pizza everyone wants a bite of.

Meanwhile, in Asia, Japan was busy expanding its empire. The Philippines, Singapore, and Burma were all swept up in the tide of war.

It was as if Japan was playing a game of Pac-Man, gobbling up territories individually.

Entry of the United States into the War

Now, let's turn our attention to the United States. For the early part of the war, the U.S. was like a kid watching a playground fight from a safe distance. But when Japan attacked Pearl Harbor in 1941, it was like a sucker punch to the gut. The U.S. was suddenly thrust into the center of the conflict.

President Franklin D. Roosevelt called December 7, 1941, "a date which will live in infamy." It was a wake-up call, like a loud alarm clock startling you awake. The U.S. declared war on Japan, and because Italy and Germany were allies of Japan, the U.S. also declared war on them. The playground observer was now in the thick of the fight.

The Holocaust and its Horrors

While soldiers fought on the battlefields, another kind of horror was unfolding in Europe. It was the Holocaust, a word that would come to represent one of the darkest chapters in human history.

Under Hitler's rule, six million Jews were systematically murdered. It's a number so large that it's hard to grasp. Wonder that every person in Los Angeles. Now, all of them are gone. That's what six million looks like.

The Nazis, Hitler's party, also targeted other groups they considered undesirable. This included Romani people, disabled individuals, Poles, Soviet prisoners of war, and many others. Concentration camps and ghettos were set up across Europe. These were not like the summer camps you might be thinking of. They were places of unspeakable cruelty and suffering.

The Holocaust was a stark reminder of the depths to which humanity can sink. It was a tragedy of unimaginable proportions. But even in the midst of such darkness, there were rays of light. Individuals who risked their lives to save others. Stories of bravery, resilience, and humanity that shone like stars in the night sky.

As we delve deeper into World War II, we'll encounter such stories – tales of individuals who stood up against injustice, showed courage in the face of fear and dared to hope in times of despair. These stories remind us that the human spirit can shine brightly even in the darkest times.

So, as we turn the page on this chapter of our historical adventure, remember the lessons we've learned. The causes of war are complex and multifaceted. Its impacts are far-reaching and profound. But in the midst of conflict, there are always stories of hope, bravery, and resilience. Stories that inspire us to be better, to do better, to strive for a world where peace prevails.

So, let's remember, let's learn, and let's continue our adventure. There's a lot more history to uncover, a lot more stories to discover, and a lot more lessons to learn. Onward, young historians! The journey continues.

"*I say that the delivery of needed supplies to Britain is imperative. I say that this can be done; it must be done; and it will be done...The only thing we have to fear is fear itself.*"

– Franklin D. Roosevelt, May 1941

CHAPTER 2:
The Skies of War - Battles Above and Beyond

Have you ever had a dream where you're flying high in the sky, soaring like a bird, wind in your hair, freedom in your heart? Envision that feeling, but now add in the roar of engines, the chatter over the radio, and the knowledge that you are miles above the earth in a powerful machine of metal and might. Exciting, right? But now, you can think that you're not alone in the sky. There are others, and they're not there to enjoy the view. They're there to fight.

This was the reality for the pilots during World War II, a reality we're about to dive into as we take our historical exploration to new heights. So, strap in, hold on tight, and prepare for sky-high adventures!

2.1 The Battle of Britain: Sky Wars

Reflect this: It's the summer of 1940, and Britain stands alone against the powerful German forces. It's like being the last player on your team during a dodgeball game, facing an onslaught of flying balls. The Battle of Britain was about to begin and would be a fight for the skies.

The Luftwaffe vs the Royal Air Force

The Luftwaffe, Germany's air force, was a formidable opponent. Vision a swarm of angry hornets, each one fast, powerful, and deadly. That was the Luftwaffe. They had modern aircraft, experienced pilots, and a successful track record in Poland and France. They were ready to bring the war to Britain's doorstep.

On the other side was the Royal Air Force (RAF), Britain's own band of airborne warriors. They were fewer in number, but they were not to be underestimated. You know that saying, "It's not the size of the dog in the fight, it's the size of the fight in the dog"? That was the RAF. They were determined, they were brave, and they were ready to defend their skies.

The Importance of Radar Technology

But how do you defend against an enemy that can come from any direction at any time? Well, the British had a secret weapon - radar. The same radar that helps predict weather and track ships at sea was Britain's early warning system against incoming German aircraft.

Radar stations along the coast would detect incoming aircraft, and the information would be relayed to Fighter Command, which would then scramble its fighters. It was like having a lookout in a game of hide and seek, giving the RAF precious minutes to get their planes in the air.

And it wasn't just the technology, but how they used it. The British developed a system called the Dowding System, named after Air Chief Marshal Hugh Dowding. This system integrated radar detection, ground observation, and fighter dispatch into one coordinated system. It was like the body's nervous system, reacting quickly and efficiently to threats.

The Resilience of the British People

While the battle raged in the skies, the people of Britain held their breath on the ground. The German strategy was not just to defeat the RAF but to break the will of the British people through sustained bombing raids, known as The Blitz.

But the British people were made of stern stuff. They faced the bombings with a spirit of endurance and defiance known as the "Blitz Spirit." It was as if they were saying to the Germans, "Is that the best you can do?" They took cover during the air raids, helped each other out of the rubble, and continued their lives. It was this resilience and courage that saw them through the Battle of Britain and, ultimately, helped them win.

So, there's our first foray into the battles of World War II. We've soared high in the skies with the pilots of the RAF, felt the tension of a radar operator as blips appeared on the screen, and stood shoulder to shoulder with the stalwart British public as they faced the Blitz. It's been a thrilling ride, but we're not done yet. There are more battles to explore and more stories to discover. So, stay tuned, history buffs. Our adventure continues!

2.2 The Pearl Harbor Attack: A Day of Infamy

Reflect the essence of a calm Sunday morning. The sun is shining, the skies are clear, and you're looking forward to a day of rest and relaxation. Now, that tranquility was shattered by the roar of aircraft engines and the deafening boom of explosions. This was the reality for the servicemen and civilians at Pearl Harbor on December 7, 1941.

Japan's Surprise Attack on the U.S. Naval Base

The Pacific Ocean seems vast, doesn't it? It's so big that you'd think it impossible for anyone to cross it undetected. But with careful planning

Chapter 2: The Skies of War - Battles Above and Beyond

and a dose of audacity, that's exactly what the Japanese did. Like a tiger stalking its prey, they crept closer, careful not to give away their position.

The strike was timed to perfection, early on a Sunday morning, when the base was most relaxed. The first wave of Japanese aircraft swooped down on the unsuspecting base, dropping their bombs and torpedoes with deadly accuracy. It was like a swarm of wasps, buzzing in to sting before you even knew what was happening.

The Sinking of the USS Arizona

Among the ships moored at Pearl Harbor that day was the USS Arizona, a proud battleship of the U.S. Pacific Fleet. Visualize the giant of steel and power, a floating fortress bristling with guns. That was the Arizona.

But even giants can fall. A bomb dropped from a Japanese plane found its mark, piercing the deck and igniting the ammunition stored below. The resulting explosion was catastrophic, ripping the ship apart and sending it to the bottom of the harbor. It was a devastating blow, a symbol of the surprise and ferocity of the attack.

U.S. Declaration of War on Japan

In the aftermath of the attack, the United States was a nation in shock. Imagine the disbelief, the outrage, the burning desire for justice. Japan had not only attacked them but had done so while peace talks were still ongoing. It was like being punched in the face while shaking hands.

President Franklin D. Roosevelt addressed the nation and the world, declaring December 7, 1941, a "date which will live in infamy." With those words, he echoed the sentiment of millions of Americans - this was a day they would never forget.

The following day, the United States declared war on Japan. Like a sleeping giant rudely awakened, they were now fully thrust into the global conflict. Their entry marked a significant turning point in World War II.

And so, the tranquil Pacific became a battleground, a theatre of war where, once again, courage and resilience would be tested. The attack on Pearl Harbor is a stark reminder of the unpredictability of war and the devastation it can bring. It also highlights the resolve of nations and individuals in the face of adversity. From the ruins of the attack rose a determined America, ready to fight for freedom and justice.

So, as we continue to navigate the vast narrative of World War II, let's keep in mind the lessons we've learned so far. War is unpredictable, and its consequences are far-reaching. Yet, even in adversity, the human spirit remains unbroken, rising to confront the challenges with courage and resilience.

2.3 The D-Day Invasion: Turning the Tide

You're playing a game of chess. You're losing, but you have one last trick up your sleeve. You've been planning it for months, waiting for the perfect moment. Now, it's time to make your move. That's what the D-Day Invasion was for the Allies - a carefully planned operation that would turn the tide of World War II.

Planning of Operation Overlord

Behind the scenes, top military brass from the Allies plotted a massive assault, an operation so significant it could change the course of the war. They named it Operation Overlord, a name as grand as the plan itself.

Picture a group of military leaders huddled over maps, discussing strategies, and making critical decisions. They had to consider everything from the weather to the tides, from the strength of the German defenses to the element of surprise. It was like planning the world's most complicated surprise party, only with much more at stake.

The Landing on Normandy Beaches

June 6, 1944, marked the day of the invasion. Instead of birthday candles and party poppers, soldiers geared up for the largest seaborne invasion in history. Reflect on the calm like the early morning mist, the hum of thousands of engines, and the determined faces of the soldiers. As the sun rose, the beaches of Normandy were about to become a stage for heroism and tragedy.

The landing was a massive operation involving over 156,000 troops across five beach sectors: Utah, Omaha, Gold, Juno, and Sword. Imagine a stretch of sand, quiet and serene one moment and a chaotic battleground the next. Soldiers braved the hail of bullets and shellfire, charging through the surf, scrambling up the beaches, their hearts filled with determination and courage.

The Liberation of Paris

The Allies gained a crucial foothold with the successful landing at Normandy. But the fight was far from over. Envision a giant domino setup. The landing was just the first domino to fall, setting off a chain reaction that would lead to the liberation of Paris.

Paris, the City of Lights, had been under German occupation since 1940. Wonder that the once-vibrant city, its lights dimmed, its spirit subdued but not broken. Parisians had been waiting, hoping, and praying for liberation. And finally, on August 25, 1944, their prayers were answered.

As Allied troops marched through the streets of Paris, jubilant crowds greeted them with tears, cheers, and a collective sigh of relief. The Eiffel Tower, once a symbol of German occupation, now stood as a beacon of hope and freedom.

So, there you have it - a glimpse into one of the most significant operations of World War II. The D-Day Invasion was a testament to strategic planning, bravery, and the collective will of nations united against a common enemy. It showed that even in the face of immense challenges, victory is possible when people come together for a common cause. From the planning stages of Operation Overlord to the triumphant liberation of Paris, each moment, each decision, and each action played a crucial role in turning the tide of the war.

2.4 The Battle of the Bulge: A Surprise Attack

Let's zero in on a frosty winter day in December 1944. Picture soldiers huddled around makeshift campfires, their breath fogging up in the chilly air, a white blanket of snow covering the ground. In the quiet of the Ardennes forest, an unexpected storm was brewing, not of snow and ice but of steel and fire. This was the eve of the Battle of the Bulge, Germany's last roll of the dice in World War II.

Germany's last major offensive

Consider a soccer game. Your team is behind, the clock is ticking, and you need a goal to turn the game around. That's the kind of desperate situation Germany found itself in towards the end of 1944. With the Allies advancing steadily, Adolf Hitler launched a surprise counteroffensive.

Nicknamed the 'Battle of the Bulge' for the westward bulge it created in the Allied front lines, this assault was Germany's attempt to cut off and destroy large parts of the Allied forces. Imagine a snake trying to constrict its prey—that's what Germany aimed to do. It was a risky gamble, but Hitler was willing to take that chance.

The Siege of Bastogne

One of the key locations during this battle was the small town of Bastogne in Belgium. Visualize the atmosphere of a tiny island surrounded by a sea of enemy forces. Bastogne was like that island, a strategic crossroads surrounded by the German army on all sides.

The 101st Airborne Division of the U.S. Army defended the city. Outnumbered and surrounded, these men were stuck in a dire situation, like a mouse cornered by a cat. But they refused to give in. When the Germans sent a message asking for their surrender, the acting commander, Brigadier General Anthony McAuliffe, sent back a one-word reply: "Nuts!" It was a defiant response that echoed the spirit of resistance among the Allies.

The turning point of the war in Europe
The Battle of the Bulge was a brutal encounter, with both sides facing heavy losses. But ultimately, it marked a significant turning point in the war. Envision reaching the top of a steep hill, panting and tired but also relieved because now you only have to go downhill. That's how the Allies must have felt.

Despite the initial surprise, the Allies regrouped and pushed back the German forces. Picture a wall of water crashing against a dam, straining against the concrete, threatening to break through. And then, the dam holds, the water recedes, and the crisis is averted. That's what it was like when the Allies halted the German advance.

Bastogne's successful defense played a crucial role in this. Reinforcements arrived, the weather improved, and the Allied air forces, now able to take to the skies, started attacking the German supply lines. It was like the sun breaking through the clouds after a fierce storm, turning the tide in favor of the Allies.

In the aftermath of the battle, the German forces were left weakened and demoralized. Their last-ditch attempt to turn the war around had failed. It was only a matter of time before the Allies would cross the Rhine and invade Germany.

So, there you have it, folks! A whirlwind tour of the Battle of the Bulge. We've walked in the boots of the brave soldiers in the snowy trenches, felt the tension in the besieged town of Bastogne, and witnessed the decisive turn of the tide in the Allies' favor. These stories and experiences are not just relics of a bygone era. They're reminders of our human capacity for courage, resilience, and hope, even in the face of overwhelming odds.

So, keep these lessons in mind as we forge ahead. There's plenty more to explore, more battles to relive, more heroes to meet. The past awaits, and our quest for knowledge continues. Until next time, stay curious, stay brave, and keep those history gears turning!

"Our citizens can now rejoice that a momentous victory is in the making. Perhaps we will be forgiven if we claim we are about midway to our objective."

– Fleet Admiral Chester W. Nimitz, June 1942

CHAPTER 3:
Life on the Homefront - The Hidden Heroes of War

For a moment, visualize you standing on the moon, looking down at the Earth. From up there, our planet looks peaceful, calm, and incredibly beautiful. But if you could zoom in, like using a telescope, you'd see a different idea. The period of World War II was anything but peaceful. It was a time of chaos, destruction, and uncertainty. Still, amidst all this, life had to go on. Today, we will explore life for those not on the battlefields but on the home front.

3.1 Life in a World at War
Blackouts and air raid drills

Imagine you're at home, and suddenly, all the lights go out. It's pitch black, and you can't see a thing. That's what blackouts were like during World War II. But instead of a power cut, these blackouts were deliberate. All across Britain, the lights would go out every night as soon as the sunset. Not just in homes but in streets, factories, and businesses too.

You might be wondering, why would they do this? Well, it made it difficult for enemy bombers to find their targets. Think of it as a giant hide-and-seek game in the dark. But this was no game. The stakes were very high. During these blackouts, families would gather in their homes, listening to the drone of enemy aircraft and the distant boom of bombs.

Alongside blackouts, air raid drills became a regular part of life. Think of a schoolyard where, instead of fire drills, students practiced for air raids. They were taught to duck, cover, and protect themselves from falling debris. It was a strange and frightening time, but also a time when communities came together, supporting each other through the shared experience.

Propaganda and its role in shaping public opinion
Now, let's talk about propaganda. Imagine you're reading a comic book, but instead of superheroes, it's filled with stories about how great your country is and how terrible the enemy is. That's what propaganda was like during World War II.

Governments used propaganda to boost morale, encourage people to support the war effort, and shape public opinion. Posters, films, radio broadcasts, and even comic books were used to spread certain ideas and messages. It was like being in a play where the government was the director, telling people how to think and feel about the war.

For example, in Britain, posters with slogans like "Keep Calm and Carry On" and "Your Courage, Your Cheerfulness, Your Resolution Will Bring Us Victory" were common. These messages aimed to keep spirits high and foster unity and resilience among the people.

The role of radio in connecting people
In a time before the internet and smartphones, radio was the primary source of news and entertainment. Suppose a family huddled around a radio set, listening to news bulletins, music, and comedy shows. The

radio was like a lifeline, a window to the world, keeping people connected and informed.

During the war, radio broadcasts played a crucial role. They provided updates on the progress of the war, delivered important announcements, and helped keep morale high with music and entertainment programs. For many, the radio was a trusted companion, a source of comfort, and a beacon of hope in challenging times.

The BBC, in particular, played a vital role in Britain. Its broadcasts not only reached homes across the country but also across the world. The BBC's World Service became a vital news source for people living in occupied countries. It was like a thread, weaving together stories from around the globe, keeping people informed, and providing a sense of unity in a world at war.

So, as you can see, life on the home front was a mix of normal everyday activities, new routines, and collective efforts to support the war. Through blackouts and air raid drills, propaganda, and radio broadcasts, people adapted, endured, and played their part in the war. It was a time of change, of challenges, and of resilience, offering us lessons of courage, unity, and the indomitable human spirit.

3.2 Rationing and Victory Gardens

The Introduction of Ration Books

Think of a world where every morsel of food, every drop of fuel, and every thread of cloth is accounted for. Sounds pretty strict, right? That's exactly what life was like during World War II due to rationing. Don't confuse this with rationing your Halloween candy to make it last longer. This was a whole different level.

Governments worldwide issued ration books, which were like meal tickets for the entire population. Each person was given a book filled with coupons. These coupons were exchanged for food, clothing, and other essential items. Think of it as shopping, but you pay with tiny pieces of paper instead of cash.

The idea behind rationing was to ensure that everyone got their fair share. With so much of the country's resources going towards the war effort, there simply wasn't enough to go around. Rationing was a way to keep things balanced and ensure no one went without. It was like a giant game of even stars, where everyone gets an equal slice of the pie.

Growing Vegetables at Home in Victory Gardens
Now, Envision you're at home and decide to plant a vegetable garden in your backyard. You're probably thinking, "Well, that sounds like a fun hobby!" But during World War II, gardening was more than just a hobby; it was a patriotic duty.

People were encouraged to plant "Victory Gardens," small vegetable plots in their yards, parks, and even on rooftops. Envision rows of carrots, tomatoes, and potatoes, all growing in a place where flowers or grass might have been before. These gardens were like mini grocery stores, providing fresh produce right at home.

Victory Gardens were a way for people to contribute to the war effort and supplement their rations. They also served as a morale booster, giving people a sense of purpose and control in a time of uncertainty. It was like being part of a huge team, where everyone plays their part for the win.

The Importance of Recycling and Conservation
During World War II, recycling wasn't just an eco-friendly trend but a necessity. With resources being stretched to the limit, nothing could go to waste. Envision a world where every scrap of metal, every piece of paper, and every drop of used cooking oil was collected and repurposed.

People were encouraged to conserve resources in every way possible. This meant mending old clothes instead of buying new ones, walking or cycling instead of driving, and saving leftovers instead of throwing them away. It was a time of make-do-and-mend, a time when less was definitely more.

Recycling and conservation were not just about saving resources; they were about supporting the troops. The materials collected were used to make weapons, vehicles, and other equipment for the war. By recycling, people directly contributed to the war effort, helping their country from the comfort of their homes.

So, as you can see, life on the home front during World War II was a delicate balance of rationing, recycling, and resilience. The war touched every aspect of daily life, from the pages of ration books to the rows of Victory Gardens. Yet, through these challenges, people found ways to contribute, adapt and persevere. Their efforts, often unseen and unsung, played a crucial role in the broader tapestry of the war, reminding us that everyone, in their own way, can make a difference.

3.3 The Role of Women and Children

Women in Factories: The Rise of "Rosie the Riveter"

Imagine the sights of your mom, sister, or friend. Now imagine her wearing overalls, her hair tucked under a bandana, standing proudly in front of a factory machine. During World War II, this was the reality for millions of women. With men away fighting, women stepped in to fill their shoes at home.

One of the most iconic representations of these working women was "Rosie the Riveter," a fictional character who appeared on a U.S. government poster with the slogan "We Can Do It!" Rosie was strong, confident, and capable. She was like a superhero; she wore a factory uniform instead of a cape.

Rosie symbolizes the women who worked in factories, producing everything from bullets to bombers. These women were essential to the war effort. They worked long hours, often in difficult conditions, but they did it with a sense of pride and purpose. It was like they were in the trenches, not with guns, but with wrenches, playing their part in the fight for freedom.

Children's War Efforts: Collecting Scrap Metal and Growing Victory Gardens

Now, let's turn our attention to the younger members of society. Children, too, played their part in the war effort. Reflect school kids learning about history and being a part of it. Children contributed in many ways, from collecting scrap metal to growing Victory Gardens.

Think of a schoolyard turned into a mini recycling center. Children would bring in old pots, pans, and any other scrap metal they could find. These collections were then used to make weapons and other war materials. It was like a school project, only on a much larger scale and with a greater purpose.

Children also played a part in the Victory Garden movement. They would help plant and tend gardens at home or school, learning about plants while contributing to the food supply. It was like a science class, and a life lesson rolled into one.

The Evacuation of Children in Britain

Now, let's take a moment to think about a different aspect of life during the war - the evacuation of children. Picture a train station filled with children, their faces a mix of excitement, anxiety, and confusion. This was the scene in Britain at the start of the war.

With the threat of air raids looming, the British government decided to move children from cities to the countryside. Imagine being a child, saying goodbye to your parents, not knowing when you would see them again. It was a hard decision, but it was made to keep the children safe.

These evacuations were like a massive sleepover without fun and games. Children were sent to live with host families, adjusting to new homes, new schools, and a new way of life. Despite the challenges, these children showed remarkable resilience. They adapted, made the best of the situation, and carried on.

So, the war was not just fought on the battlefield. It was also fought on the factory floors, in the schoolyards, and in the hearts and minds of the people at home. Women and children, often overlooked in the history books, played crucial roles in the war effort. Their contributions, sacrifices, and resilience are integral to the story of World War II.

So, as we delve deeper into the tales of the war, let's remember these unsung heroes. Let's celebrate their courage, their determination, and their spirit. They, too, were a part of this great historical saga, playing their part, making a difference, and leaving their mark on history.

3.4 Stories of Hope and Resilience
The Story of Anne Frank

A secret hideaway in a quiet neighborhood in Amsterdam was nestled behind a bookcase. A young girl named Anne Frank and her family found refuge in this hidden annex. Now, picture yourself in Anne's shoes. You're confined in a small space, away from your friends and the outside world, with only the blank pages of your diary for company. This was Anne's world from 1942 to 1944, hiding from the Nazis who had occupied the Netherlands.

Anne's diary, a gift for her 13th birthday, became her confidante and companion. She filled its pages with her thoughts, dreams, fears, and observations about life in the annex. Imagine pouring your heart into a diary, unaware that your words would one day touch the hearts of millions worldwide.

Despite the fear and uncertainty, Anne's spirit remained unbroken. She wrote about her belief in the goodness of people, her hope for a better future, and her dreams of becoming a writer. Her words were like rays of sunshine piercing through the darkness of the war. Even in the face of adversity, Anne showed us the power of hope, the strength of the human spirit, and the enduring resonance of a young girl's dream.

The Bravery of Soldiers on the Front Lines
Now, let's turn our attention to the soldiers on the front lines. I wonder about the adventure as a soldier who is far from home and faces danger and uncertainty daily. Yet, despite the fear and hardships, these brave individuals showed exceptional courage and resilience.

Think about the soldiers storming the beaches of Normandy on D-Day, facing a hail of gunfire as they charged toward an uncertain fate. Or consider the servicemen at Pearl Harbor, responding with bravery and determination in the face of a surprise attack. These soldiers were like knights from the old stories, facing dragons and danger with courage and honor.

Each soldier had their own story, reasons for fighting, hopes, and dreams. Their bravery was not just about winning battles or earning medals. It was about standing up for their beliefs, defending their homes, and protecting their loved ones. It was about the resilience of the human spirit, the will to endure, and the courage to fight for a better world.

The Resilience of Civilians on the Home Front
Back home, civilians were doing their part to support the war effort. See yourself in a neighborhood transformed by the war. Air raid sirens and blackouts become a part of your daily routine. The local park is

now a Victory Garden; your school collects scrap metal. This was the reality for civilians during World War II.

Despite the challenges, the spirit of the people remained strong. They adapted to the changes, found contributing ways, and carried on with determination and resilience. They were like tree roots, holding strong and providing support even in the face of a storm.

Women stepped into new roles, working in factories and contributing to the war effort. Children helped, too, collecting scrap metal and growing vegetables in Victory Gardens. Despite the fear and uncertainty, people opened their hearts and homes to evacuate children, providing them with safety and care.

These stories of hope and resilience remind us that the human spirit remains strong even in the toughest of times. Whether it's a young girl writing in her diary, a soldier charging into battle, or a civilian planting a Victory Garden, each person plays a part in the tapestry of war. Their stories are a testament to the courage, strength, and resilience that lie within each of us.

In these tales from the home front, we see the echoes of our own lives. We see the challenges we face, the changes we navigate, and the resilience we demonstrate. We see the power of hope, community strength, and humanity's enduring spirit. As we continue to explore the many facets of World War II, let these stories inspire you, uplift you, and remind you of the extraordinary potential within each of us.

"Wars may be fought with weapons, but they are won by men. It is the spirit of men who follow and of the man who leads that gains the victory."

– General George S. Patton, September 1933

CHAPTER 4:
Unlikely Heroes: Ordinary People in Extraordinary Times

If I told you that a farm boy would become one of World War II's most decorated American soldiers, would you believe me? Or, would you be surprised if I said that a young man from a humble background would rise to receive every military combat award for valor available from the U.S. Army? Well, let's dive into the incredible story of Audie Murphy, a young man whose life turned from ordinary to extraordinary through the crucible of war.

4.1 The Story of Audie Murphy: From Farm Boy to Hero
Early Life and Enlistment
Envision a scrawny, dirt-smudged boy with a resolute gaze working tirelessly on a farm in Texas. This was Audie Murphy, the son of poor sharecroppers, who had to quit school in the fifth grade to support his family. Life was hard, but Murphy was harder. He was no stranger to long hours, grueling work, and the harsh realities of life.

However, working on the farm wasn't the life Murphy dreamed of. He yearned for something more, for a chance to serve his country. He tried to enlist in the military after the attack on Pearl Harbor but was turned away for being underage. But, like a cat eyeing a canary, Murphy was patient and persistent. On his 18th birthday, he enlisted in the Army, stepping into a journey that would transform his life.

Distinguished Service

Murphy's transition was anything but easy from the farm fields of Texas to the battlefields of Europe. He was often underestimated because of his small stature and quiet demeanor. But, like a diamond in the rough, Murphy's true mettle shone through in the heat of battle.

Murphy fought in several major campaigns during the war, proving himself a skilled and brave soldier. But his actions in the Battle of Holtzwihr in January 1945 elevated him to a hero. Murphy, a young lieutenant, single-handedly holds off an entire company of German soldiers. Despite a leg injury, he climbed aboard a burning tank destroyer and used its machine gun to hold off the enemy. It was like a scene straight out of an action movie, only this was real life, and the stakes were higher than any Hollywood script.

This heroic stand earned Murphy the Medal of Honor, the highest military decoration awarded by the United States. But he didn't stop there. By the war's end, Murphy had received a staggering 33 awards and decorations, making him one of the most decorated American soldiers of World War II.

Post-War Life and Legacy

After the war, Murphy's life took another unexpected turn. From the battlefields of Europe, he stepped into the glitz and glamour of Hollywood. See yourself trading your military uniform for costumes and your battlefield comrades for co-stars. That's what Murphy did, becoming a successful actor and starring in more than 40 films.

But, like many veterans, Murphy struggled with the invisible scars of war. He had what we now recognize as Post Traumatic Stress Disorder (PTSD). Despite the challenges he faced, Murphy used his fame to bring attention to the struggles of veterans, advocating for better mental health care for soldiers returning from war.

Audie Murphy's life was a testament to the power of courage, resilience, and determination. From a farm boy in Texas to a war hero and a Hollywood star, he showed us that heroes often come from the most unlikely places. His story serves as a reminder that ordinary people are capable of extraordinary bravery and selflessness.

So, as we explore more stories of unlikely heroes, let's remember Audie Murphy. Let's remember his courage, his sacrifice, and his legacy. And let's remember that within us lies the potential for greatness, the potential to rise above our circumstances, and the potential to make a difference in the world.

4.2 The Navajo Code Talkers: Secret Messengers
Recruitment and Training

Imagine being a teenager living in the vast, sun-drenched landscapes of the Navajo Nation. Your days are filled with the rhythm of tradition, the language of your ancestors rolling off your tongue. Suddenly, World War II erupts, and you're enlisted into a unique battalion where your native language is your most potent weapon. This was the reality for the Navajo Code Talkers.

The U.S. Marines, recognizing the potential of the complex Navajo language, recruited young Navajo men. Their language, unwritten and known only to its own people, was an enigma to outsiders. Let yourself drift into a secret club with a code that no one else can crack; that was the Navajo language to the rest of the world.

In the military camps, the recruits underwent rigorous training. They were not only taught standard military protocols but also given the task of developing a new code using their native language. It was like creating a secret handshake, only far more complicated and with much higher stakes.

Role in the Pacific Theater

Now, let's transport ourselves to the volatile battlegrounds of the Pacific Theater. The Navajo Code Talkers were assigned to Marine units fighting in the Pacific, and their role was crucial and clear - to communicate important messages on tactics, troop movements, and orders without the enemy deciphering the content.

Visualize a chaotic battlefield, explosions rocking the ground, bullets whizzing past, and amidst this bedlam, the calm voice of a Code Talker relaying coded messages over a field radio. Based on the Navajo language, their codes were a mystery to the Japanese forces, who were left confused.

The Code Talkers participated in every major operation involving the U.S. Marines in the Pacific, their voices cutting through the fog of war, providing clarity and direction. Their codes were never broken, a testament to their complexity and the skill of the Code Talkers. Like a ship's compass in a storm, they guided the Marines, their contributions invaluable and instrumental in winning the war.

Recognition and Legacy

Fast forward to the end of the war, and the Navajo Code Talkers returned home as unsung heroes. Their incredible efforts remained a military secret until 1968, when their code was finally declassified. Envision saving a goal during a soccer game but not being allowed to tell anyone about it for over two decades; that's how the Code Talkers must have felt.

In 2001, the Navajo Code Talkers were awarded the Congressional Gold Medal, the highest civilian honor in the United States. Allow your mind to wander the pride and joy on their faces as they finally received the recognition they deserved, their heroism no longer a secret but a celebrated piece of history.

The Navajo Code Talkers are a shining reminder that heroes come in many forms and that sometimes, the most powerful weapon can be a language spoken by a few. Their legacy lives on, a testament to the strength of their spirit, the power of their language, and their unwavering dedication to their country.

So, let's carry forth the story of the Navajo Code Talkers, etching their heroism into our minds and their legacy into our hearts. As we continue to explore the annals of World War II, let these unlikely heroes inspire us, reminding us that we all possess the potential for greatness, irrespective of who we are or where we come from.

4.3 The Tuskegee Airmen: Breaking Barriers
Formation of the Squadron

Let's take flight with a group of trailblazing pilots, the Tuskegee Airmen, who soared above societal norms to etch their names in history. Feel yourself in a time when segregation was the norm in the United States, a time when the color of your skin limited your dreams. This was the world in which the Tuskegee Airmen dared to dream of flying.

Established in 1941, the Tuskegee Airmen were a group of African American military pilots trained at Tuskegee Army Airfield in Alabama. They were pioneers, shattering the glass ceiling that had long kept them grounded. Imagine standing at the foot of a mountain, gazing up at the summit, knowing that you're about to make the climb. That's how these men must have felt.

Missions and Achievements

From the skies over North Africa to the heart of Europe, the Tuskegee Airmen took on some of the war's most dangerous and critical missions. Transport yourself to a team of football players, underdogs who are not expected to win, yet they play with such skill and determination that they leave everyone astounded. That was the Tuskegee Airmen.

Their valor shone brightly in the heat of battle, successfully escorting countless bomber missions over Europe. Their reputation was such that bomber crews often requested them as escorts, knowing they were in capable hands under the Tuskegee Airmen's watch. Their red-tailed aircraft became a beacon of hope and protection in the hostile skies.

Impact on Racial Integration in the Military

The impact of the Tuskegee Airmen extended far beyond the battlefields. Their bravery and excellence challenged biases, broke down barriers, and paved the way for the desegregation of the U.S. military in 1948. Imagine a wall, a barrier that has long stood, finally crumbling down. The Tuskegee Airmen were instrumental in bringing that wall down.

The Tuskegee Airmen are a testament to the power of perseverance and the strength of the human spirit. Their story is about courage, determination, and a relentless pursuit of equality. As we continue our exploration of World War II, let's remember the Tuskegee Airmen, their red-tailed planes a symbol of bravery, a beacon of change, and a testament to the belief that the sky's the limit, no matter who you are.

4.4 The Story of Nancy Wake: The White Mouse
Early Life and Resistance Work

Let's now journey to the vibrant streets of Paris in the 1930s, where a young woman named Nancy Wake lived a life of adventure and glamour. Wake was a force to be reckoned with with her flaming red hair and lively spirit. But as war clouds gathered over Europe, her life took a dramatic turn.

Wake was living in Marseille with her French husband when the war broke out. Rather than retreating to the safety of her native Australia, she chose to stay and fight. Ideate standing at a fork in the road, knowing that one path leads to safety and the other to danger. Wake chose the latter, and in doing so, she embarked on a path of resistance and espionage that would earn her the nickname "The White Mouse."

Espionage and Sabotage Operations

Wake joined the French Resistance, a network of individuals and groups who fought against the German occupation and the Vichy regime. Step into the scene of a chess game played not on a board but in the shadows. That's what life was like in the Resistance: a dangerous game of strategy, cunning, and nerve.

Her operations included espionage, sabotage, and even leading attacks against German installations. Imagine a spy movie filled with coded messages, secret rendezvous, and daring escapes. Wake's reality was a world of danger, intrigue, and courage.

Despite being high on the Gestapo's most-wanted list, Wake managed to evade capture. Her elusive nature and ability to slip through the fingers of the Gestapo earned her the nickname "The White Mouse." She was like a ghost, unseen and untouchable, always one step ahead of her pursuers.

Post-War Recognition and Legacy

After the war, Wake was decorated with numerous honors, including the George Medal, the United States Medal of Freedom, the Médaille de la Résistance, and three Croix de Guerre. See yourself a hero standing tall, her chest adorned with medals, each a reminder of her courage, service, and unwavering spirit.

Wake's story is a testament to the power of courage, resistance, and resilience. Her actions during the war were instrumental in undermining the German occupation in France, and her legacy continues to inspire people worldwide. As we delve deeper into the stories of World War II, let's keep in mind the courage and determination of individuals like Nancy Wake. Their actions remind us that heroes can come from all walks of life and that each one of us has the potential to make a difference.

The tales explored in this chapter remind us that heroism comes in many forms and that sometimes, the most unlikely individuals can have the most profound impact. As we continue our exploration of World War II, let's carry forth these stories of courage, resilience, and hope, drawing inspiration from their deeds and learning from their experiences. Each story is a piece of the larger puzzle, a thread in the vast tapestry of history, and a testament to the extraordinary potential within each of us. So, let's press on, eager to discover what lies ahead.

"We shall not fail or falter; we shall not weaken or tire. Neither the sudden shock of battle, nor the long-drawn trials of vigilance and exertion will wear us down."

– Prime Minister Winston Churchill, February 1941

CHAPTER 5:
Unheard Voices and Unseen Heroes

Envision yourself standing in a world shrouded in darkness, where the sun rarely seems to peek through the heavy clouds. Yet, amidst this dark and gloomy landscape are flashes of light, moments of extraordinary bravery and compassion that illuminate the shadows. These stories often go untold, the stories of unsung heroes whose courage and selflessness remind us of the enduring spirit of humanity. In this chapter, we'll delve into such stories, exploring the lives of individuals who dared to challenge the status quo, stand up against oppression, and make a difference in their own unique ways.

5.1 The Story of Irena Sendler: Life in a Jar
Life in Occupied Poland
Wonder that a bustling city suddenly silenced, and its vibrant streets turned into a grim tableau of fear and oppression. This was the reality of Warsaw, Poland, following the Nazi invasion during World War II. Amidst this bleak landscape, a beacon of hope emerged from a courageous woman named Irena Sendler.

A social worker by profession, Irena was a regular sight in the beleaguered Warsaw Ghetto, where thousands of Jewish families were confined in squalid conditions. Think of a single rose blooming amidst a field of thorns—that was Irena, her compassion and determination a stark contrast to the cruelty surrounding her.

Rescue Operations and Arrest
Despite the danger, Irena, along with her network of allies, embarked on a daring mission to rescue Jewish children from the Ghetto. Visualize yourself in a chess game against a formidable opponent, where every move carries immense risk and the potential for significant gain. That was the dangerous dance Irena and her team were engaged in.

Using her position as a social worker as a cover, Irena masterminded the smuggling of children out of the Ghetto, placing them with Polish families or in orphanages. Imagine carrying a small, terrified child in your arms, knowing that you're their only hope for survival. Irena bore This heavy burden, which she carried with unwavering dedication and courage.

Irena's operation was eventually discovered, and the Gestapo arrested her. Despite enduring torture, she refused to betray her comrades or the children she had saved. Despite such adversity, Irena's resilience was like a steel beam, unbending and unyielding.

Recognition and Legacy
Irena survived the war, but her heroic deeds remained largely unrecognized until the early 2000s when a group of Kansas high school students discovered her story and created a play titled "Life in a Jar." Step into the scene of a spotlight suddenly illuminating a forgotten heroine on the stage of history—that was the effect of this simple school project.

Today, Irena Sendler is celebrated as a hero, and her story is a powerful reminder of the difference one person can make. She was nominated for the Nobel Peace Prize and honored by international organizations for her selfless service. But perhaps the most poignant tribute to Irena's legacy is the survival and success of the children she rescued; their lives are a testament to her courage, compassion, and indomitable spirit.

As we delve deeper into the stories of unsung heroes, let's carry Irena's tale in our hearts. Her story teaches us that even in the darkest times, there is always a place for kindness, bravery, and compassion. It shows us that one person can make a profound difference in the world no matter how ordinary they may seem.

5.2 The Story of Chiune Sugihara: The Japanese Schindler
Diplomatic Career and Decision to Help

The Japanese consulate stood in the heart of Lithuania, nestled amongst cobbled streets and quaint houses. At its helm was Chiune Sugihara, a man whose life was about to take an extraordinary turn. Let's dream about a calm lake, its surface undisturbed until a single pebble is thrown in, creating ripples that spread across the entire lake. For Sugihara, his pebble moment came with the onset of World War II.

As a diplomat, Sugihara was skilled in negotiations and a master in the art of conversation. He had a knack for navigating complex situations with grace and tact. But nothing could have prepared him for what was to come. With the war escalating and Jewish refugees pouring into Lithuania, Sugihara faced a moral dilemma that would change his life and the lives of thousands of others.

As the desperate pleas for help grew, Sugihara made a decision. A decision to help, to stand up against the tide of injustice, to throw his own pebble into the lake. He decided to issue transit visas to Jewish refugees, allowing them to travel through Japan to escape the horrors of the Holocaust.

Issuing of Visas and Consequences

In the face of a looming humanitarian crisis, Sugihara began to write visas. Allow your mind to wander to a man hunched over his desk, pen in hand, writing for hours on end, each stroke of his pen a lifeline for a desperate refugee. Sugihara was that man. He wrote thousands of visas, his hands cramping, his eyes weary, but his spirit unbroken.

However, his actions came at a great cost. Issuing these visas was a clear violation of his government's orders. Contemplate a tightrope walker, carefully balancing on the rope, aware that one wrong step could lead to a fall. Sugihara was that tightrope walker and his actions put his career and family's future at risk.

Despite the consequences, Sugihara continued to write visas until the very last moment, even throwing visas from the train window as he was leaving Lithuania. His selfless actions saved the lives of around 6,000 Jews, a feat that earned him the nickname "The Japanese Schindler."

Post-War Life and Honors

As the dust of war settled, Sugihara's life took a downturn. He was asked to resign from his post, and his career as a diplomat abruptly ended due to his wartime actions. Picture a warrior returning home from battle only to find his home in ruins. Sugihara's return to Japan was marked with hardship and obscurity.

However, his story was far from over. His deeds came to light many years later, and the world began to acknowledge his heroic actions. Take a moment to think about a sun slowly rising above the horizon, its light gradually illuminating the world. Sugihara's recognition was much like that sunrise, slow but inevitable.

In 1985, Israel honored Sugihara as "Righteous Among the Nations," a title given to non-Jews who risked their lives to save Jews during the Holocaust. Place yourself in a man standing tall as he receives his honor and his actions are finally acknowledged and celebrated.

The life of Chiune Sugihara is a testament to the power of compassion, courage, and conviction. His story reminds us that in the face of injustice, we have the power to make a difference. Every visa Sugihara wrote, every life he saved, was a step towards a more compassionate world. His legacy continues to inspire, reminding us that even in the darkest times, there are always rays of hope, always individuals ready to stand up for what is right.

5.3 The Story of the White Rose: Voices of Resistance
Formation and Ideals

Imagine a group of young university students, their heads filled with ideas, their hearts brimming with courage. This was the White Rose, a non-violent resistance group in Nazi Germany. Visualize a delicate white rose, a symbol of purity and innocence, standing tall amidst the thorny brambles of oppression and fear. That was the image the group embodied, their name a beacon of hope in a time of despair.

The core members of the White Rose were five students and a professor from the University of Munich. They were Sophie and Hans Scholl, Alex Schmorell, Willi Graf, Christoph Probst, and Professor Kurt Huber. Picture a band of friends, bound not just by shared interests or common pursuits but by a shared conviction to fight for justice and freedom.

The White Rose believed in the power of words to fight against the tyranny of the Nazi regime. They were like poets on a battlefield: their pens, swords, swords, and shields. Their ideals were deeply rooted in their Christian beliefs and faith in human dignity. They believed that every individual had the right to think and act freely, a right that was being crushed under the heel of the Nazi regime.

Distribution of Leaflets and Arrest

Armed with their ideals and their courage, the members of the White Rose embarked on a daring mission to spread the truth about the Nazi regime. They decided to publish and distribute leaflets that criticized the Nazis and called for resistance. Let's dream about a flock of birds carrying messages tied to their feet, flying across the city, dropping their messages into the laps of unsuspecting citizens. That's what the distribution of leaflets was like. Only instead of birds, it was the members of the White Rose, and instead of messages, it was the truth about the Nazi regime.

However, their operations were fraught with danger. The Gestapo, the secret police of the Nazi regime, was always on the lookout for dissenters. Transport yourself standing near a cat, its eyes sharp, its claws ready, waiting to pounce on the unsuspecting mouse. That was the Gestapo, and the members of the White Rose were their targets.

Despite the risks, the White Rose distributed thousands of leaflets across Germany. However, their operation was eventually discovered. In February 1943, Hans and Sophie Scholl were caught distributing leaflets at the University of Munich. They were arrested, along with other members of the White Rose, and executed for treason. Visualize a candle being snuffed out, its light suddenly extinguished. That was the fate of the White Rose, their voices silenced but not forgotten.

Impact and Legacy

The story of the White Rose did not end with their arrest. Their legacy lived on, their courage echoing through the corridors of history. Picture a pebble thrown into a lake, creating ripples that spread far and wide.

The White Rose was that pebble, their actions creating ripples that would resonate across Germany and the world.

Their leaflets were smuggled out of Germany and air-dropped over the country by Allied planes. Their words reached millions, awakening a sense of outrage and a desire for resistance. The White Rose became a symbol of peaceful resistance against the Nazi regime, their story inspiring others to stand up against injustice and oppression.

Today, the members of the White Rose are honored as heroes in Germany. Schools, streets, and squares have been named after them, and their story is taught in schools. See yourself amid a group of children sitting in a classroom named after Sophie Scholl, learning about the courage and sacrifice of the White Rose. That is the legacy of the White Rose, their spirit living on in the hearts and minds of future generations.

The story of the White Rose is a powerful testament to the courage and resilience of ordinary individuals in extraordinary times. It reminds us that the human spirit cannot be crushed even in the face of brutal oppression. Their legacy continues to inspire us, a reminder that every voice matters and that even the smallest act of resistance can spark a movement for change. As we navigate the complex narratives of World War II, let's carry the story of the White Rose in our hearts: their courage, their guiding light, their legacy, and their inspiration.

5.4 The Story of Noor Inayat Khan: The Spy Princess
Early Life and Recruitment
Born into Indian royalty and raised in the heart of Paris, Noor Inayat Khan led an enchanting life. Picture a child listening to tales of her ancestral heritage as the descendant of Tipu Sultan, the Tiger of Mysore, while also soaking in the vibrant culture of the City of Lights. This was Noor's childhood, a blend of Eastern heritage and Western influence.

However, Noor's life's tranquil rhythm was disrupted by World War II's onset. As the dark shadow of Nazi occupation fell over Paris, Noor and her family fled to England. Here, Noor's life would take an unexpected turn.

In England, Noor felt the call to serve her adopted home. Her French proficiency and daring spirit caught the attention of the Special Operations Executive (SOE), a British organization tasked with espionage and sabotage in occupied Europe. Envision this moment as a chess player carefully plotting their next move. That was Noor, as she boldly decided to join the SOE, stepping onto a path of danger, intrigue, and heroism.

Espionage Work and Capture

Trained as a wireless operator, Noor was deployed back into occupied France. Imagine being dropped into a lion's den, knowing every move could be your last. That was the reality Noor faced, operating undercover in a hostile environment.

Despite the risks, Noor was a model agent, transmitting crucial information while evading capture. See yourself amid a whisper in the wind, conveying a message without revealing its source. That was Noor, her stealth and courage baffling the enemy.

However, the danger was always one step behind. Noor's operation was compromised, and the Gestapo captured her. Yet, even in captivity, Noor's spirit remained unbroken. She made multiple escape attempts and refused to reveal any information, her resilience a shining beacon in the face of adversity.

Posthumous Recognition and Legacy

Tragically, Noor's story does not have a happy ending. She was executed at Dachau concentration camp in 1944, her life cut short, but her legacy is immortal. Contemplate is surrounded by a star burning brightly before fading into the darkness. That was Noor; her life was a brilliant flash of courage and sacrifice.

In the years following the war, Noor's heroism was recognized and celebrated. She was posthumously awarded the George Cross by Britain and the Croix de Guerre by France, the highest honors of both nations. Picture a medal gleaming brightly, symbolizing a hero's courage and sacrifice. That was Noor's recognition, a testament to her bravery and dedication.

Today, Noor Inayat Khan's story continues to inspire. Her courage, resilience, and unwavering commitment to her cause remind us that heroes come in all forms. Noor was a spy, not just a war hero, but also a symbol of hope and resistance. Her story is a beacon of light, shining through the darkest times, inspiring us to stand up for what we believe in and to fight for a better world.

And so, we close this chapter, but the stories of these unsung heroes continue to resonate within us. Their courage, resilience, and selflessness serve as a constant reminder of the extraordinary feats ordinary individuals can achieve. As we navigate the complexities of our own lives, let's keep their stories alive in our hearts, drawing inspiration from their bravery and determination. And as we turn the page, let's carry their spirit with us, ready to meet the challenges ahead with the same courage and resilience they demonstrated.

"What counts is not the size of the dog in the fight—it's the size of the fight in the dog."

– President Dwight D. Eisenhower, January 1958

CHAPTER 6:
The Furry and Feathered Heroes of World War II

Deliberate a pigeon, a dog, and another dog walking into a bar. No, this isn't the start of a joke, but the beginning of an intriguing chapter of our World War II journey. These animals, often seen as mere pets or even pests, stepped up in the most extraordinary ways during the war. They were the unsung heroes, their stories as fascinating as they are heartwarming.

6.1 The Story of G.I. Joe: The Pigeon That Saved Lives
Training and Service

Think about a pigeon. You're probably picturing a city square full of cooing birds pecking at breadcrumbs. Now, reimagine these pigeons as vital messengers during World War II. One such pigeon was G.I. Joe.

G.I. Joe was no ordinary bird but a U.S. Army Pigeon Service member. He was trained to carry crucial messages across enemy lines. Illuminate a boot camp but for birds. That was G.I. Joe's training ground. He learned to fly faster, navigate better, and become the best bird he could be.

The Crucial Mission

The actual test came in October 1943. British troops were planning to attack the German-occupied Italian town of Colvi Vecchia. However, the Allies had already captured the city, and the British air attack was unnecessary.

The problem? The only way to relay this message in time was G.I. Joe. Visualize a race against time, with lives hanging in the balance. G.I. Joe was released 20 miles from the air base. He had to reach it in 20 minutes to prevent the attack. It was like an intense sports match, the clock ticking down, the crowd on the edge of their seats.

Honors and Retirement

Against all odds, G.I. Joe made it in time, saving the lives of at least 100 Allied soldiers. Imagine the relief and the cheers as the message arrived, just as the planes prepared for takeoff. G.I. Joe wasn't just a pigeon; he was a hero.

In 1946, G.I. Joe was awarded the Dickin Medal, the animal equivalent of the Victoria Cross, for his heroic service. Consider the sensations of a proud pigeon standing tall with a medal placed around his neck. That was G.I. Joe, an unlikely hero of World War II.

After the war, G.I. Joe retired to the U.S. Army's Churchill Loft at Fort Monmouth, where he lived until he died in 1961. His body was preserved and displayed at the U.S. Army Communications-Electronics Museum in Fort Monmouth, New Jersey. So, the next time you see a pigeon in the park, remember G.I. Joe, the feathered hero who soared above and beyond the call of duty.

6.2 The Story of Chips: The Dog Who Fought a War

Enlistment and Training

Now, let's drift our attention towards a lively young pup named Chips, a German Shepherd-Collie-Siberian Husky mix. Picture a scene of absolute domestic bliss, a playful dog frolicking in the yard, a loving family watching with smiles of delight. That was Chips, living an ordinary life with the Wren family in New York. But soon, he was to swap his cozy life for a military collar.

When the U.S. entered the war, the Wrens enlisted Chips into Dogs for Defense, a program initiated to train domestic dogs for war service. Visualize a rambunctious young pup shifting gears from chasing balls to undergoing rigorous training. Chips learned to become a sentry dog and was trained to alert his handlers to any strangers or changes in the environment.

Heroic Actions and Awards

Fast forward to 1943 on a beach in Sicily. The air is thick with tension as Allied forces invade. Amidst the chaos, Chips breaks free from his handlers and dashes towards a machine gun nest. Picture the scene: a brave dog charging without any thought for his own safety. Chips attacked the enemy soldiers, forcing them to surrender. His courageous act saved the lives of his entire platoon and helped the Allies secure the beach.

Chips didn't stop there. Throughout his service, he proved his mettle, sniffing out enemy soldiers and alerting his handlers to potential threats. Much like a trusted scout, Chips used his keen senses to protect his fellow soldiers, his actions speaking louder than any medal or citation.

Chips was awarded the Silver Star for Valor and the Purple Heart for his bravery. However, these medals were revoked due to an Army policy preventing official commendation of animals. Still, in the hearts of those he served with, Chips remained a decorated hero.

Post-War Life and Legacy

When the echoes of war finally faded, Chips returned to his family in New York. He traded his military collar for a comfortable pet's life, enjoying his well-deserved rest. But Chips was more than just a pet; he was a war hero, a testament to the power of loyalty and courage.

Though Chips passed away a few years after the war, his story continues to inspire. In 2018, he was posthumously awarded the Dickin Medal, known as the animal equivalent of the Victoria Cross. Imagine a shining medal, a symbol of heroism and bravery, awarded to a dog who went above and beyond the call of duty.

The tale of Chips serves as a reminder of the unsung heroes of the war, the ones who barked instead of speaking, who wagged their tails instead of shaking hands. Often overlooked in the grand scheme of things, their contributions played a pivotal role in shaping the war's course. From the courageous charge of Chips to the tireless service of countless other animals, these stories highlight the profound impact of our furry and feathered friends. Amidst the tales of human bravery and sacrifice, let's not forget these unlikely heroes who served with nothing but unwavering loyalty and courage. Their stories are a testament to the bond between humans and animals, a bond that can indeed change the course of history.

6.3 The Story of Antis: The Brave Dog in the Skies
Early Life and Adoption

Consider the sensations of the sprawling landscapes of Czechoslovakia in the late 1930s. Amidst the tranquil countryside, we find a young German Shepherd pup named Antis, unaware of the extraordinary life ahead. Much like a blank canvas waiting to be painted with the hues of life, Antis was on the brink of an adventure that would color his life with acts of courage and loyalty.

Antis was found by Robert Bozdech, a Czech airman, during a bombing mission in France. Just imagine a tiny, scared pup in the midst of chaos and destruction, rescued by a kind-hearted airman, and a moment of serendipity marked the beginning of an unbreakable bond between the two. Bozdech, taken by the pup's spirit, decided to adopt him, unknowingly welcoming a future war hero into his life.

Service in the Air Force
Fast forward to the heart of World War II. As Bozdech found himself serving in the British Royal Air Force, so did Antis. Consider a German Shepherd, not chasing balls or sticks but flying high in the belly of a bomber plane. Antis was right beside Bozdech, braving the thundering engines, the high altitudes, and the perilous missions.

Unlike regular Air Force members, Antis had no formal training. Yet, he adapted to his unique life with the tenacity and bravery characteristic of his breed. He flew on numerous missions with Bozdech, and his presence was a comforting constant for the airman amidst the uncertainty of war. Deliberate a loyal companion standing by your side, unfazed by the dangers, providing a sense of solace and normalcy in a world turned upside down. That was Antis for Bozdech.

Antis's keen senses proved invaluable on multiple occasions. His acute hearing and sharp bark alerted airfield personnel to approaching enemy aircraft, saving countless lives. Picture a dog, not barking at a squirrel or a passing car, but at incoming enemy bombers, his warnings a crucial line of defense.

Post-War Life and Recognition
As the echoes of war faded, both Bozdech and Antis returned to a quieter life. Recall going from the roaring engines of a bomber plane to the soft humming of a peaceful household. Antis faced this transition,

yet he took it in his stride, adapting to his post-war life with the same courage he displayed during the war.

The extraordinary tale of Antis did not go unnoticed. In 1949, Antis was awarded the Dickin Medal, often called the Victoria Cross for animals. Picture a shiny medal glistening in the sunlight, a symbol of valor and bravery hung around the neck of a German Shepherd. That was the honor bestowed upon Antis, a recognition of his service and heroism.

Antis's story continues to inspire and captivate. His bravery, loyalty, and unwavering spirit testify to animals' significant role in World War II. As we navigate the vast narrative of the war, let's remember Antis, a dog who soared above his call of duty and proved that heroes come in all shapes, sizes, and even species.

6.4 The Story of Judy: The Dog that Became a Prisoner of War
Early Life and Naval Service

Illuminate an energetic puppy bounding across the fields of Shanghai in the early 1930s. This lively pup was Judy, an English Pointer who was about to step paw-first into an extraordinary life. Judy found her calling when the British gunboat HMS Gnat crew adopted her. Visualize a furry, four-legged sailor, her tail wagging in the sea breeze, her eyes sparkling excitedly. That was Judy, sailing the high seas, her heart filled with the spirit of adventure.

Serving aboard a ship wasn't just fun and games for Judy. She had duties to perform, from catching rats to providing companionship to the crew. Judy took to her naval life like a fish to water, and her keen senses and loyal nature proved invaluable to her shipmates. Think about a ship on a stormy sea, the crew working tirelessly against the raging elements, and amidst them, a dog standing firm, her presence a comforting constant. That was Judy's spirit as unyielding as the ship she served on.

Capture and Life in Prison Camp

As the storm of World War II swept across the globe, Judy and her crew found themselves in the thick of the conflict. When their ship was sunk by Japanese planes, Judy didn't panic. Instead, she helped save the crew's lives, nudging them towards pieces of wreckage to hold onto. Picture a furry lifeguard, her eyes scanning the water, her body diving through the waves to rescue her friends. That was Judy, a beacon of hope amidst the chaos.

But the trials for Judy were far from over. She was captured along with her crew and taken to a Japanese prisoner-of-war camp. Visualize the magic of a grim, fenced enclosure, its occupants worn down by the harsh conditions. Yet, amidst this bleak landscape, Judy's spirit remained unbroken. She comforted the prisoners, her wagging tail and friendly nuzzles bringing fleeting moments of joy into their grim existence.

Judy's courage shone through in the camp. She would growl and bark at the guards when they threatened the prisoners, her protective instincts coming to the fore. Imagine a small dog standing her ground against armed guards, her body tense, her eyes blazing. That was Judy, fearless and protective, her loyalty to her crew unwavering even in the face of danger.

Post-War Life and Honors

When the war ended, Judy's trials weren't over. She had to be smuggled out of the camp to ensure her safety, a task that her fellow prisoner and caretaker, Leading Aircraftman Frank Williams, took upon himself. Picture a daring escape, a man and his loyal dog evading the watchful eyes of their captors, their hearts pounding with fear and exhilaration. That was Frank and Judy; their bond was more vital than ever, and their spirit was unbroken.

Once back in Britain, Judy was greeted with joy and relief. She spent the rest of her days in the peaceful countryside, a far cry from the war-torn landscapes she had braved. Consider this scenario: a content dog basking in the sun, her body relaxed, her heart at peace. That was Judy, her spirit finally at rest, her days of hardship behind her.

In recognition of her bravery, Judy was awarded the Dickin Medal in 1946. Picture a medal gleaming in the sunlight, its ribbon the color of bravery hung around the neck of a dog. That was Judy, a war hero; her courage was finally recognized and honored.

The tale of Judy, the dog that became a prisoner of war, is a testament to the indomitable spirit of animals and their profound bond with humans. Her story serves as a reminder of the unsung heroes of the war, the ones who wagged their tails instead of saluting, who barked instead of speaking, yet served with nothing but unwavering loyalty and courage. As we turn the pages of history, remember these furry and feathered heroes, their stories as inspiring and significant as their human counterparts.

Indeed, bravery has many faces, and courage knows no bounds. From the feathered wings of G.I. Joe to the furry paws of Chips, from the unwavering spirit of Antis to the indomitable heart of Judy, we've encountered heroes who have redefined our understanding of courage and resilience. As we carry their stories in our hearts, let's step forward into the next chapter of our exploration, ready to uncover more tales of bravery, stories of courage, and heroes that history often forgets.

"We have known the bitterness of defeat and the exultation of triumph, and from both we have learned there can be no turning back. We must go forward to preserve in peace what we won in war."

– General Douglas MacArthur, September 1945

CHAPTER 7:
The Dawn After Darkness: The End of World War II and the Birth of a New Era

Picture a long, cold winter where the sun seems to have hidden away, the days are filled with biting cold, and the nights are longer than ever. Now, Imagine the first day of spring, when the sun finally peeks out from behind the clouds, and the air is filled with relief and the promise of warmth. This is what the end of World War II was like for many around the globe: a long-awaited spring following a harsh and seemingly endless winter.

The end of World War II wasn't just about the cessation of fighting; it was about picking up the pieces, healing, and starting anew. It was about seeking justice and laying the foundation for a peaceful future. The war's conclusion brought about significant events that shaped the rest of the 20th century. So, let's step into this pivotal time in history when the world collectively sighed in relief and started to rebuild.

7.1 Victory in Europe (VE) Day: The End of Fighting in Europe
The Announcement of Germany's Surrender
The year 1945 greeted the world with the news it had been waiting for: the end of the war in Europe. Imagine turning on the radio one morning

and hearing the announcement that Germany had surrendered. This was the news that millions woke up to on May 7, 1945. The long and bloody conflict that had ravaged Europe was finally coming to an end.

Germany's unconditional surrender marked the collapse of Hitler's Third Reich. Consider this scenario: a towering fortress, once seeming invincible, has now fallen into ruins. That was the state of Nazi Germany, its dreams of world domination shattered, its leaders defeated or dead, and its people left to grapple with the aftermath of a devastating war.

Public Celebrations in Allied Countries

As news of Germany's surrender spread, spontaneous celebrations erupted in Allied nations. Transport your thoughts to the streets of London, Paris, and New York, filled with jubilant crowds, the air thick with relief and joy. People were dancing in the streets, hugging each other, and crying tears of happiness. The long nightmare was finally over, and the world had survived.

These celebrations were about victory over the enemy, survival, and resilience. They were about the countless lives saved, the homes that would no longer be bombed, and the families that could now hope for a peaceful future. It was a moment of collective joy that the world had been yearning for.

Churchill's Famous Speech

On VE Day, British Prime Minister Winston Churchill delivered a historic speech to a jubilant London crowd and listeners worldwide via radio broadcast. Picture the charismatic Churchill standing on a balcony overlooking the cheering crowds, his voice carrying the weight of a hard-won victory and the relief of a nation.

In his speech, Churchill paid tribute to the bravery and sacrifice of the armed forces and ordinary citizens who had endured six years of war. But he also cautioned that the war was not entirely over, with Japan still needing to be defeated. His words captured the mixed feelings of the time—a joyous relief at the end of fighting in Europe but a recognition that the path to global peace was not fully cleared yet.

The end of World War II in Europe marked a critical turning point in history. It brought relief and jubilation but also ushered in a time of reflection and reckoning. It was a period of endings and beginnings, of closure and renewal. As we delve further into this fascinating period, we'll explore the significant events that followed the war's end in Europe, which continued to shape our world for years to come.

7.2 Victory over Japan (VJ) Day: The End of World War II

The Dropping of Atomic Bombs on Hiroshima and Nagasaki

The sun rose over the city of Hiroshima on the morning of August 6, 1945, its residents unaware that the day would end unlike any other. High above the city, a B-29 bomber named Enola Gay released "Little Boy," the first atomic bomb. The city was decimated, its buildings reduced to rubble, its people to shadows. Picture a city going about its daily routine, and everything instantly changes. That was Hiroshima on that fateful day.

Just three days later, another bomb, "Fat Man," was dropped on the city of Nagasaki. Illuminate a thunderstorm with lightning that doesn't just flash and disappear but lingers, scorching everything in its path. That was the reality of Nagasaki in the aftermath of the bombing.

This marked a terrifying chapter in human history—the use of nuclear weapons in warfare. The bombings resulted in immense destruction and loss of life, the shockwaves of which are felt to this day. It demonstrated the devastating power humanity now wielded, a power that would forever change the nature of global conflict.

Japan's Official Surrender Aboard the USS Missouri

The atomic bombings signaled the endgame of World War II. Barely a week later, on August 15, 1945, Japan announced its surrender, bringing the brutal and destructive war to a close. Picture a game of chess and the king finally cornered, with no moves left to make. That was the situation Japan found itself in, its surrender marking the end of World War II.

The official surrender ceremony took place on September 2, 1945, aboard the USS Missouri, anchored in Tokyo Bay. Transport yourself to the solemn faces of the Japanese delegates as they signed the Instrument of Surrender, the hushed silence only broken by the scratch of pen on paper. It was a moment of closure, a moment that marked the end of a bloody chapter in human history.

The Impact on the Pacific Region

The end of World War II brought about a significant transformation in the Pacific region. The once mighty Japanese Empire was dismantled, and its colonies gained independence or transitioned into new forms of governance. Imagine a giant jigsaw puzzle, its pieces scattered and then put together in a completely different way. That was the Pacific region in the aftermath of the war; the map was redrawn, and the balance of power shifted.

The war's impact was political, deeply social, and cultural. Countries ravaged by the war had to rebuild from the ruins, heal the wounds of conflict, and reconcile with their past. Picture a phoenix rising from the ashes, ready to soar into the sky. That was the Pacific region, its people demonstrating a resilience and determination that would see them navigate the challenges of the post-war period and lay the foundations for a future of peace and prosperity.

As we delve into this critical period of history, let's remember the lessons it teaches us—the horrors of war, the resilience of the human spirit, and the enduring hope for a peaceful future. These lessons, gleaned from the end of World War II, serve as a reminder of our past and a guide for our future.

7.3 The Nuremberg Trials: A Fight for Justice

The Establishment of the International Military Tribunal

As the curtain fell on the World War II stage, the spotlight turned to a new setting: a courtroom in Nuremberg, Germany. Picture a grand hall, its walls echoing the whispers of justice, its seats filled with men and women who had the daunting task of holding war criminals accountable. This was the birthplace of the International Military Tribunal (IMT), a court specifically convened to try the major war criminals of the European Axis countries.

The IMT was a joint venture, a collaborative effort by the four major Allied powers: the United States, Britain, the Soviet Union, and France. Imagine a team of rivals, each with their own strategies and tactics, coming together for a common cause. The IMT was a symbol of cooperation in the pursuit of justice, a testament to the shared values and goals of the Allied nations.

The charter of the IMT was adopted in August 1945. It outlined the laws and procedures for the trials, establishing the legal framework within which justice would be served. Picture a blueprint, not for a building, but for a legal process that would set precedents for international law.

Key Figures Who Were Tried and Their Sentences

The Nuremberg trials were not just ordinary court proceedings. They were the stage where some of the most infamous figures of the Nazi regime faced justice. Imagine a parade of men, not in uniforms or regalia, but as defendants in a court of law. From Hermann Göring, Hitler's designated successor, to Rudolf Hess, the deputy Führer, the trials brought together key figures of the Nazi leadership.

The charges were severe and included crimes against peace, war crimes, and crimes against humanity. Consider this scenario: a scale not weighing gold or silver, but the weight of crimes so heinous they're difficult to comprehend. The verdicts handed down by the IMT were a reflection of this weight.

Of the 24 defendants, 12 were sentenced to death, seven received prison sentences, and three were acquitted. Ideate the fall of a judge's gavel, each strike a blow for justice, each sentence a message to the world that such atrocities would not go unpunished.

The Significance of the Trials in International Law

The Nuremberg Trials were not just about punishing the guilty; they were about setting a precedent for international law. Picture a path through a dense forest, the underbrush cleared to reveal a new way forward. The trials were a pathfinder, charting a new course for how the world handles war crimes and crimes against humanity.

The principles established at Nuremberg formed the basis for our international laws today, including the concept of "crimes against humanity." Illuminate a rulebook, not for a game but for the conduct of nations and individuals during times of war. The trials contributed to this rulebook, their impact resonating in courtrooms around the world.

Furthermore, the trials led to the establishment of the International Court of Justice and the International Criminal Court. These institutions stand as pillars of justice in the international community, their foundations laid in the aftermath of World War II.

The phoenix of justice rose from the ashes of war, its wings spreading over Nuremberg as the trials progressed. The legacy of these trials continues to shape our world, their principles etched into the bedrock of international law. As we navigate the intricate narratives of World War II, we come to appreciate the significance of the Nuremberg Trials, their place in history, and their impact on our present.

7.4 The Formation of the United Nations: A Hope for Peace

The Drafting of the UN Charter

Envision this: It's 1945, and representatives from 50 countries gather in San Francisco. It's not a festival or a convention; it's a conference with a mission. Their objective? To draft the United Nations Charter, a pivotal document that would serve as the backbone of a new world organization. Like architects, they discussed, debated, and meticulously designed the blueprint for a more peaceful world.

Project the hum of voices in the room, the air thick with anticipation and determination. These delegates, representing diverse nations and cultures, were united by a common purpose: to prevent future wars, to promote human rights, and to foster social progress. The UN Charter, inked with the aspirations of these nations, was more than just a document; it was a beacon of hope in a world emerging from the shadows of war.

The Establishment of the General Assembly and Security Council

With the Charter as their guide, the United Nations began to take shape. At its heart were two key components: the General Assembly and the Security Council. Picture a tree, its branches representing the various member nations, all connected to the strong trunk of the United Nations. The General Assembly and Security Council were like the roots of this tree, providing stability and nourishment.

The General Assembly was like a global town hall where all member nations had a seat and a voice. Here, countries big and small, near and far, could express their views, discuss global issues, and work towards consensus.

The Security Council, on the other hand, was like the guardians of peace. Tasked with maintaining international security, it had five permanent members with veto power and ten elected members. In this council chamber, decisions that could tip the scales of global peace were made, and its members were entrusted with the heavy responsibility of preventing conflicts and preserving harmony.

The Universal Declaration of Human Rights

In the aftermath of a war that had witnessed unspeakable atrocities, the United Nations rose to the challenge of protecting and promoting human rights. See yourself amid a world wearies of war, its people yearning for safety, dignity, and equal rights. For this world, the Universal Declaration of Human Rights promised that everyone, regardless of race, religion, or nationality, would be treated with respect and dignity.

The Declaration, adopted by the General Assembly in 1948, was a milestone in human history. For the first time, it set out fundamental human rights to be universally protected. Like a parent setting out rules for their children, the Declaration established the basic principles of equality, freedom, and justice that every nation should uphold.

The formation of the United Nations marked a turning point in global history. It was a testament to humanity's ability to rise from the ashes of war and strive for a better, more peaceful world. The UN Charter, the General Assembly, the Security Council, and the Universal Declaration of Human Rights were the cornerstones of a new world.

As we explore the aftermath of World War II, let's remember the pivotal role played by the United Nations. Its formation was a beacon of hope in a time of uncertainty, and its mission was a testament to humanity's enduring aspiration for peace. With the echoes of war still lingering, the world was on a path of reconstruction and reconciliation, a path illuminated by the ideals of the United Nations.

This chapter has taken us through the end of the most devastating conflict in human history and the birth of a new era of global cooperation. We've seen the world rise from the ashes of war and take the first steps towards a more peaceful future. But our exploration doesn't end here. As we turn the page, we'll delve into how the world remembered World War II and how it continues to shape our present. So, keep those history gears turning. There are more tales to uncover, lessons to learn, and heroes to remember!

"If I had foreseen Hiroshima and Nagasaki, I would have torn up my formula in 1905."

– Albert Einstein, 1948

CHAPTER 8:
Echoes of the Past: The Importance of Remembering World War II

Close your eyes. Explore like you're standing in front of a vast ocean. You toss a pebble into the water. It creates ripples that extend far beyond the point of impact, touching distant shores. This is much like the effects of World War II, a significant event that sent ripples through time and continues to influence our world today. But why is it so crucial to remember this war? Why should we retell these stories of heroism, survival, and change? Let's find out.

8.1 The Importance of Remembrance
Honoring the Sacrifices of Soldiers and Civilians
Picture a marathon runner, their muscles straining, their breath ragged, but their eyes fixed on the finish line. That's what the soldiers and civilians who lived through World War II were like. They endured hardship, faced unimaginable challenges, and made immense sacrifices. Some gave their time and resources, while others gave something even more precious—their lives.

Remembering World War II is a way for us to honor these individuals. It's like giving a standing ovation to a performer after a spectacular performance to show our respect and gratitude. By learning about their experiences, we pay tribute to their courage and resilience, ensuring that their sacrifices are not forgotten.

Learning from Past Mistakes
Now, imagine you're in a maze. You take a wrong turn and hit a dead-end. What do you do next? You backtrack and find a new path, making sure not to repeat the same mistake. Remembering World War II serves a similar purpose. It's our way of looking back at past mistakes to avoid repeating them in the future.

From the rise of totalitarian regimes to the horrors of the Holocaust, World War II is filled with lessons on what can happen when hate and intolerance are allowed to flourish. We remind ourselves of our world's need for vigilance, empathy, and justice by remembering these events. It's like a lighthouse guiding a ship, helping us navigate the complex waters of the present.

Fostering a Sense of Shared History
Think of a family reunion, where stories are shared over a meal, creating a sense of connection and belonging. Remembering World War II has a similar effect on a global scale. It helps foster a sense of shared history, reminding us that we are all part of a larger human family.

The war affected millions of people from diverse backgrounds. It touched every continent, crossed cultural and linguistic barriers, and altered the course of countless lives. By exploring these experiences, we acknowledge our shared past, understand our present, and shape our future. It's like weaving a tapestry, where each thread—each story—adds to a larger, more complex picture of our world.

So, let's remember World War II. Let's honor the sacrifices of the soldiers and civilians, learn from past mistakes, and foster a sense of shared history. Let's keep the ripples of this significant event alive in our collective memory, touching the shores of our present and future. Remembering is not just about looking back; it's about moving forward with a broader perspective and a deeper understanding of our world.

8.2 World War II Memorials Around the World

The National World War II Memorial in Washington, D.C.

Imagine standing in the heart of the United States' capital amidst the hustle and bustle of city life, a serene space dedicated to the valor and unity of a nation emerges. This is the National World War II Memorial in Washington, D.C. Picture a grand monument, its granite pillars standing tall, each representing a U.S. state or territory from the period of the war. Between these pillars, a pool reflects the Lincoln Memorial, symbolizing the ideals the war fought to defend.

This memorial isn't just about stone and water but about the stories etched into its very fabric. Inscribed on its Freedom Wall are 4,048 gold stars, each one representing 100 American lives lost in the war. Contemplate each star as a silent tribute, a golden testament to the sacrifices made for the cause of freedom. This is a place of reflection, where the echoes of the past resonate with the hopes of the present.

The Soviet War Memorial in Berlin

Now, let's traverse continents and land in the heart of Berlin, where a different memorial stands. This is the Soviet War Memorial, a monument dedicated to the 80,000 Soviet soldiers who fell in the Battle of Berlin. Picture a massive bronze soldier, his sword lowered over a broken swastika, a symbol of victory over the Nazi regime.

Like a time capsule, this memorial captures the poignant moments of a city caught in the throes of war. It is a testament to the courage and resilience of the soldiers who fought against the darkness of fascism. This memorial reminds us that the road to peace is often paved with sacrifices and that every step toward a brighter future is built on the lessons of the past.

The Hiroshima Peace Memorial Park in Japan
Finally, let's journey to the Land of the Rising Sun, a city that rose from the ashes of destruction. Hiroshima, once devastated by an atomic bomb, is now a city of peace, its transformation symbolized by the Hiroshima Peace Memorial Park. See yourself amid a lush, tranquil park, its green expanses offering a serene space amidst the bustling cityscape.

At the heart of the park stands the Genbaku Dome, or the A-Bomb Dome, the skeletal ruins of a building that survived the atomic blast. It stands as a stark reminder of the horrors of nuclear warfare, its silent form echoing the plea for peace. Nearby, the Children's Peace Monument, a statue of a young girl holding a folded paper crane, pays tribute to the child victims of the bombing and symbolizes the hope for a peaceful future.

Each of these memorials, scattered across three continents, tells a story. They remind us of the soldiers' courage, the civilians' resilience, and the hope that emerged from the ashes of war. They are not just structures of stone and metal but symbols of our shared past, collective memory, and aspiration for a world where peace prevails. As we navigate the complexities of history, let's keep these memorials in our minds, their stories etched into our hearts, and their lessons guiding our steps toward a more peaceful future.

8.3 How World War II is Commemorated

Observance of VE Day and VJ Day

Can you hear the bells pealing in the distance, their resonant notes filling the air with a melody of joy and relief? This familiar sound echoes across many parts of the world yearly on VE (Victory in Europe) Day, celebrated on May 8, and VJ (Victory over Japan) Day, observed on August 15. These are not just dates on a calendar but significant milestones that mark the end of World War II in Europe and the Pacific.

VE Day is a time to remember the moment when the guns finally fell silent in Europe. Picture streets filled with ecstatic crowds, their faces glowing with happiness, their hearts filled with relief. That was the scene in many European cities on May 8, 1945, when Germany's surrender was officially announced.

On the other hand, VJ Day marks the day when the war ended in the Pacific. Explore like a world holding its breath, waiting for the final act of a prolonged drama to unfold. That was the world on August 15, 1945, when Japan announced its surrender, bringing the devastating conflict of World War II to a close.

Across the globe, these victories are commemorated with various events, from memorial services and military parades to moments of silence and the ringing of peace bells. These observances are poignant reminders of the joyous relief that swept across the world when the news of victory was announced. They are also an opportunity to pay tribute to the countless individuals who sacrificed their lives for the cause of freedom.

Holocaust Remembrance Day

Let's now step into a realm of memory shrouded in sorrow and resilience. Holocaust Remembrance Day, or Yom HaShoah, is observed annually, a day dedicated to the six million Jews who perished during the Holocaust. This is not a date chosen at random but corresponds to the Hebrew date of the Warsaw Ghetto Uprising in 1943, a symbol of Jewish resistance during the Holocaust.

Holocaust Remembrance Day is a time for reflection, education, and remembrance. Envision the candlelight vigils illuminating the night, their flames flickering in silent tribute to the lives lost. Imagine survivors sharing their stories, their voices a testament to their strength and resilience. This is how many around the world commemorate this day, ensuring that the victims of the Holocaust are never forgotten.

This day also serves as a stark reminder of the atrocities humans can inflict upon each other. It underscores the importance of vigilance against hatred, prejudice, and intolerance. After all, remembering the past is not just about honoring those who suffered; it's also about learning from history to build a more compassionate and peaceful future.

Pearl Harbor Day in the United States

Now, let's journey to the shores of Hawaii, where the tranquil waters of Pearl Harbor hold a tragic tale. December 7, 1941, is a date etched into the annals of history when the United States was thrust into the turmoil of World War II. Each year, on Pearl Harbor Day, Americans pause to remember the lives lost in the surprise attack by Japanese forces.

See the world as solemn ceremonies are held at the Pearl Harbor National Memorial, their backdrop the sunken USS Arizona, its wreckage a silent witness to the tragic events of that day. Project survivors, veterans, and civilians gathered together, their heads bowed in remembrance, their hearts united by a shared history. This is how the United States commemorates Pearl Harbor Day, a day of remembrance and honor for those who were killed in the attack.

As we remember these days of victory, sorrow, and shock, we are reminded of the power of commemoration. These observances are about recalling dates and events and understanding the human stories intertwined with these historical moments. They remind us of our capacity for courage, resilience, and hope, even in the face of adversity. They serve as a bridge between the past and the present, connecting us to our shared history and guiding us toward a future of peace and understanding.

8.4 Continuing the Legacy: The Role of Stories

The Use of Personal Narratives in History Education

Ideate a classroom buzzing with the chatter of eager students, their eyes glued to their history textbooks, their minds swirling with dates and events. Now, their teacher begins to tell a story, a personal narrative from World War II. Suddenly, the room falls silent, every ear tuned to the teacher's words.

You see, personal narratives aren't just stories; they are windows to the past. They enable students to step into the shoes of those who lived through the war to experience their fears, hopes, and triumphs. It's like adding a dash of color to a black-and-white photograph, making history come alive in vivid detail.

From a soldier's letter home from the front lines to a diary entry of a child in a war-torn city, these narratives are more than just primary sources. They are the threads that weave the rich tapestry of history, each one adding depth and texture to our understanding of the past.

The Impact of World War II on Literature and Film

Now, let's step into the realm of literature and film, where World War II has left an indelible mark. Picture a library shelf filled with books, each one a different tale of the war. From historical fiction to memoirs, the war has inspired countless authors, their words painting a multi-faceted portrait of this significant period.

In the world of film, World War II has been the backdrop for numerous stories, their narratives unfolding on the silver screen. Visualize a darkened cinema, the audience engrossed in a war film, their hearts pounding in sync with the on-screen action. These films transport us back in time, allowing us to experience the highs and lows of the war through the magic of cinema.

Whether it's a novel about a soldier's journey or a film depicting the home front's struggles, these stories keep the memory of World War II alive. They remind us of the human experiences behind the historical facts, ensuring that the echoes of the past continue to resonate in our present.

The Preservation of Oral Histories
Finally, let's turn our attention to oral histories, a vital part of preserving the legacy of World War II. Think of an elderly veteran whose voice is a little shaky and whose eyes are bright with memories recounting their war experiences. These oral histories are like precious heirlooms, passed down through generations, their value immeasurable.

Oral histories capture the personal experiences and reflections of those who lived through the war. They give us insight into the thoughts, emotions, and experiences that don't often make it into history books. It's like listening to a heart's whisper, each narrative revealing a piece of the human puzzle.

These stories are preserved in various ways, from recorded interviews and podcasts to documentaries and museum exhibits. They serve as a bridge from the past to the future, ensuring that the voices of World War II continue to be heard.

We continue remembering and learning from World War II through personal narratives, literature, film, and oral histories. Each story, each memory, and each voice add to our understanding of this pivotal period in our history. They remind us that behind every historical event are the stories of individuals, each contributing to our shared history's tapestry. As we continue our exploration of World War II, let's carry these stories with us, for they are not just echoes of the past but guideposts for our future. So, as we flip the page to the next chapter, let's keep our hearts and minds open to the lessons these stories have to offer.

"Never in the field of human conflict was so much owed by so many to so few."

– Prime Minister Winston Churchill, August 1940

CHAPTER 9:
Lessons of Valor: Unraveling the Teachings of World War II

9.1 Learning from the Past: The Importance of History

Reflect on navigating a maze, turning corners, hitting dead ends, and retracing your steps. Each turn teaches you something about the path, helping you find your way out. This is what history is like: a complex maze of events, decisions, and outcomes. While it may seem like we're simply revisiting the past, we're actually learning valuable lessons for our future.

The Role of History in Understanding Current Events

Consider a game of chess. The opening moves are crucial as they lay the groundwork for the game. The strategies adopted and the pieces moved contributed to the game's unfolding. Similarly, history serves as the opening moves of our present. The past's events, decisions, and actions have shaped our world today.

Let's take the formation of the United Nations as an example. As we've learned, it was a direct response to the atrocities of World War II, a global effort to prevent such a devastating conflict from happening again.

Today, the UN is critical in maintaining international peace and security, promoting human rights, and fostering social and economic development. Understanding its origin in the aftermath of World War II helps us appreciate its significance and role in our current global landscape.

The Dangers of Forgetting the Past

Now, let's go back to our maze. Project not remembering the dead ends you hit or the path that led you to them. You'd make the same mistakes, getting lost in the same corners. This is the danger of forgetting the past. We risk repeating the same mistakes if we don't remember history lessons.

Take the rise of totalitarian regimes before World War II, for instance. The world watched as democratic institutions were undermined, civil liberties were curtailed, and minorities were persecuted. The result was a devastating war that claimed millions of lives. Forgetting these events could leave us vulnerable to similar threats in the future.

The Importance of Critical Thinking in Studying History

Remember the childhood game of 'connect the dots'? It wasn't enough to simply join the dots; you had to do it correctly to reveal the true sense. Studying history requires a similar approach. We must critically analyze events, understand their causes and effects, and connect them to see the larger sense.

Let's consider the bombing of Pearl Harbor. It wasn't an isolated event but a result of escalating tensions between the United States and Japan over Japan's aggression in Asia. Understanding these underlying factors allows us to see the bombing as a surprise attack and a consequence of broader geopolitical dynamics.

So, as we navigate the maze of history, let's remember to learn from the past, be aware of the dangers of forgetting, and use critical thinking to connect the dots. These valuable skills can help us understand our world and make informed decisions about our future.

Let's carry this mindset as we explore the remaining lessons of World War II, each adding a piece to our understanding of this pivotal historical period. And remember, we're not just learning about the past; we're gathering insights for the future, ensuring that the echoes of World War II continue to guide us toward a peaceful and inclusive world.

9.2 The Power of Unity and Cooperation

Transport yourself in a group of friends coming together to build a treehouse. They each bring their unique skills and resources, working harmoniously to achieve their common goal. This sense of unity and cooperation is the cornerstone of many historical events during and after World War II.

The Formation of Alliances During the War

Let's think back to the early days of World War II. As nations were drawn into the conflict, they sought allies in their struggle against common enemies. This led to the formation of two major alliances: the Axis Powers, including Germany, Italy, and Japan, and the Allies, initially made up of Britain, France, and China, and later joined by the United States and the Soviet Union.

Imagine a group of climbers roped together as they ascend a treacherous mountain. Each climber relies on the strength and stability of the others to reach the summit. This was the essence of these wartime alliances. Shared objectives and mutual support bound them together, their combined strength greater than the sum of their parts.

The formation of these alliances played a crucial role in the war's outcome. They enabled countries to coordinate their military strategies, share resources, and support each other in adversity. It demonstrated the power of unity in overcoming shared challenges, a lesson that would prove valuable in the post-war world.

The Post-War Rebuilding Efforts

As the dust settled after World War II, the world faced the daunting task of rebuilding. Envision the experience of a city reduced to ruins, its buildings crumbled, its streets littered with rubble. Now, explore like the same city slowly returning to life, its buildings reconstructed, its streets buzzing with activity. This was the reality in many parts of the world in the aftermath of the war.

The rebuilding efforts were a testament to international cooperation. Countries came together to provide financial, technical, and humanitarian support. Consider the Marshall Plan, through which the United States provided billions of dollars in aid to help rebuild European economies. It was like a neighborhood coming together to help a family rebuild their house after a fire, demonstrating the power of collective action.

These cooperative efforts laid the groundwork for economic recovery and political stability in the post-war world. They showed that unity and cooperation could win wars and build peace.

The Creation of the European Union

In the wake of World War II, European nations sought ways to prevent another devastating conflict on their continent. This led to the European Union (EU), a unique economic and political union of European countries. Visualize the vastness of a group of neighbors agreeing to share resources, make decisions together, and resolve disputes peacefully. That was the fundamental idea behind the EU.

The establishment of the EU marked a significant milestone in international cooperation. It showed that nations could maintain their sovereignty while working together for mutual benefit. Today, the EU stands as a beacon of unity and cooperation, and its existence is a testament to the lessons learned from the tumultuous years of World War II.

Thus, from the formation of wartime alliances to post-war rebuilding efforts and the creation of the European Union, World War II and its aftermath highlight the power of unity and cooperation. These historical examples show us that we can overcome even the most daunting challenges when we work together. They remind us that unity is not just about standing together; it's about working together, making compromises, and striving for common goals. So, as we explore the lessons of World War II, let's remember the power of unity and cooperation and consider how we can apply these lessons in our own lives.

9.3 Understanding the Value of Peace
The Human Cost of World War II

Take a moment to reflect on the vast canvas of World War II. Contemplate the countless faces, each one etched with stories of courage, resilience, hope, and loss. From the soldiers who bravely fought on the front lines to the civilians whose lives were irrevocably altered by the war, each individual bore the human cost of the conflict.

The war claimed the lives of millions, the echoes of their sacrifice reverberating through time. Contemplate a sea of gravestones, each representing a life cut short, a family grieving, a future unfulfilled. The scale of loss was immense, and the impact was profound. Each life lost was a reminder of the heavy price of war, a price paid in blood and tears.

Yet, the cost was not just measured in lives lost but also in the scars carried by the survivors. Think about a soldier returning home, their body whole but their spirit wounded by the horrors they witnessed. Think of a child, their innocence lost to the harsh realities of war. These invisible wounds, these silent screams, were part of the human cost of World War II.

The Efforts to Prevent Future Wars

As the dust settled in the aftermath of the war, the world faced the daunting task of ensuring that such a catastrophe would never happen again. The collective resolve to prevent future wars led to significant efforts on multiple fronts.

Firstly, establishing the United Nations reflected the global commitment to maintaining peace and resolving conflicts through dialogue and diplomacy. Think of it as a global town hall where nations could voice their concerns, discuss issues, and work together towards common goals.

Secondly, the prosecution of war criminals in the Nuremberg Trials and subsequent tribunals was a clear signal that acts of aggression and crimes against humanity would not go unpunished. See yourself amid a courtroom, its air thick with the weight of justice being served, a message to future generations that war crimes have consequences.

Finally, the promotion of disarmament and non-aggression treaties aimed to reduce the likelihood of conflict. Picture nations not as enemies arming for battle but as partners working towards peace. These efforts were like signposts on the road to a more peaceful future, guiding the world away from the path of war.

The Role of Diplomacy in Resolving Conflicts

In the wake of World War II, diplomacy emerged as a key tool in maintaining peace and resolving conflicts. Consider how it feels in a game of chess, where strategy and negotiation are important, rather than brute force, leading to victory. Diplomacy is that game played on the global stage.

Nations could communicate their interests, address their grievances, and negotiate solutions through diplomatic channels. Reflect a roundtable where representatives of different nations sit, not with weapons but with words as their tools. This is the essence of diplomacy: bridging differences, fostering understanding, and building peaceful relations.

Moreover, diplomacy played a key role in managing tensions and preventing conflicts from escalating into full-blown wars. Visualize the atmosphere where you see a simmering pot, ready to boil over but kept in check by a careful hand. Diplomacy is that careful hand, managing the heat of international relations, preventing the pot from boiling over into the flames of war.

So, as we delve deeper into the lessons of World War II, let's keep in mind the value of peace, the efforts to prevent future wars, and the role of diplomacy in resolving conflicts. These are historical points and timeless values that continue to shape our world. They remind us that peace is not a given but a goal we must continually strive for. Through mutual understanding, cooperation, and dialogue, we can build a world where peace prevails and conflicts are resolved not on the battlefield but at the negotiating table.

9.4 The Role of Individuals in Shaping History

No discussion of World War II would be complete without acknowledging the role of individuals in shaping history. From leaders who made crucial decisions to ordinary people whose courage and resilience made a difference, World War II was a testament to the power of the individual.

The Impact of Leaders During the War

Picture a stage where leaders stand, their words echoing across nations, their decisions shaping the war's course. These leaders played a crucial role in shaping history, from Winston Churchill's rousing speeches that steeled the British resolve to President Franklin D. Roosevelt's decisive leadership that guided the United States through the war.

Yet, it was not just the leaders of the Allied forces that left their mark on history. Leaders such as Adolf Hitler, whose aggressive policies and ideologies plunged the world into war, and Emperor Hirohito, whose decision to surrender marked the end of the war in the Pacific, also played significant roles.

These leaders, with their unique leadership styles, strengths, and flaws, influenced the events of World War II. Their decisions, for better or worse, left an indelible impact on the world.

The Contributions of Ordinary People

While leaders played a significant role, the contributions of ordinary people cannot be overlooked. Picture a vast mosaic, its whole image made up of tiny pieces. Each piece is crucial to completing the whole image, no matter how small. Similarly, the story of World War II is a mosaic of millions of individual stories.

From the soldiers and airmen who fought bravely on the front lines to the workers who toiled in factories and the civilians who endured hardships on the home front, each individual played a part in the larger narrative of the war. Their courage, resilience, and sacrifices were the building blocks of history, their stories a testament to the extraordinary potential of ordinary people.

The Importance of Individual Responsibility in Society

World War II also underscored the importance of individual responsibility in society. Visualize a community where each person contributes to its well-being, and their actions shape its future. This sense of responsibility was evident during the war, as people stepped up to support the war effort in various ways.

From buying war bonds to conserving resources and volunteering for civil defense, individuals recognized their role in supporting their nations. Despite adversity, they demonstrated a sense of duty and commitment to the greater good.

Moreover, the war highlighted the consequences of apathy and indifference. The atrocities committed during the Holocaust served as a grim reminder that silence and inaction can enable injustice. It underscored the importance of standing up against oppression and defending the rights and dignity of all individuals.

As we delve deeper into the lessons of World War II, let's remember the role of individuals in shaping history. From the impact of leaders to the contributions of ordinary people and the importance of individual responsibility, these lessons remind us that we can influence the course of history. They inspire us to act courageously, uphold our responsibilities, and strive to make a difference in our world.

CONCLUSION

Well, my little time traveler, we've embarked on a whirlwind journey through the mazes and alleyways of World War II. We've swapped our time machine for a classroom seat and our explorer's hat for a thinking cap. But hey, who says learning about history can't be as thrilling as a wild adventure, right?

We've turned the pages of the past, delving into the causes of the war, the heart-stopping battles, the quiet resilience on the home front, and the big personalities that steered the course of events. We've met some extraordinary heroes on two legs, four, and even a few with wings! We've traveled from the war-weary streets of Europe to the vibrant lands of Asia, from the bustling home front to the nerve-wracking front lines.

But we found something special amidst the facts, figures, dates, and events. Can you guess what it is? No, it's not a secret treasure map or a superhero's cape. It's the inspiring stories of courage, compassion, and resilience that emerged from one of the darkest periods of our history.

We learned about the power of unity, shown by nations coming together to fight a common enemy. We saw the value of peace, etched in the sacrifices made by millions during this devastating conflict. We witnessed the role of individuals, from world leaders to everyday folks, in shaping the course of history. And yes, we also learned that even a pigeon could be a war hero!

Now, my young historian, it's your turn to take these lessons and make history yourself. No, I'm not suggesting you start a revolution or invent a time machine (though that would be pretty cool!). I'm talking about the small but powerful steps you can take daily. Stand up against injustice, lend a hand to those in need, or simply be a good friend. Each act of kindness, each stand against unfairness, is a ripple that can create waves of change. Remember, history isn't just about the past; it's about taking lessons from the past to create a better future.

As we close this book, I want you to remember that You can shape the world into a place of peace and understanding, just like the heroes we learned about. We've seen what happens when hate and intolerance take the reins. Let's envision a world steered by empathy, respect, and love. Sounds like a world you'd want to live in, right?

So, let's strive to be heroes in our own right, spreading kindness, understanding, and a dash of humor (because who doesn't need a good laugh, right?). Let's remember the past's lessons but look forward to a future where we all live in harmony. After all, if a pigeon can win a war, we can surely win the fight for a better world!

So, my little historian, are you ready for the challenge? Of course you are! Here's to a future full of peace, understanding, and a few good history books. Now, go out there and make some history!

REFERENCES

- *Causes of WW2 - World War II for Kids* https://www.ducksters.com/history/world_war_ii/causes_of_ww2.php
- *Both Mussolini's and Hitler's rise to power followed the …* https://www.hf.uio.no/iakh/english/research/news-and-events/news/2022/both-mussolinis-and-hitlers-rise-to-power
- *blitzkrieg - Students | Britannica Kids | Homework Help* https://kids.britannica.com/students/article/blitzkrieg/317670#:~:text=Blitzkrieg%20is%20a%20German%20word,to%20coordinate%20his%20own%20defenses.
- *Children and World War Two* https://www.historylearningsite.co.uk/world-war-two/children-and-world-war-two/
- *Battle of Britain Timeline: 10 July 1940 – 31 October 1940* https://bentleypriorymuseum.org.uk/bentley-priory-and-the-battle-of-britain/battle-of-britain-timeline-10-july-1940-31-october-1940/
- *Pearl Harbor: Attack, Deaths & Facts* https://www.history.com/topics/world-war-ii/pearl-harbor
- *10 Facts About D-Day You Need To Know* https://www.iwm.org.uk/history/the-10-things-you-need-to-know-about-d-day

References

- *Battle of the Bulge | Summary, Commanders, & Significance* https://www.britannica.com/event/Battle-of-the-Bulge
- *Growing Up In The Second World War* https://www.iwm.org.uk/history/growing-up-in-the-second-world-war
- *History At a Glance: Women in World War II* https://www.nationalww2museum.org/students-teachers/student-resources/research-starters/women-wwii
- *Anne Frank | Biography, Age, Death, & Facts* https://www.britannica.com/biography/Anne-Frank
- *Victory Gardens on the World War II Home Front* https://www.nps.gov/articles/000/victory-gardens-on-the-world-war-ii-home-front.htm
- *Audie Murphy - Students* https://kids.britannica.com/students/article/Audie-Murphy/330826
- *American Indian Code Talkers* https://www.nationalww2museum.org/war/articles/american-indian-code-talkers
- *How Tuskegee Airmen Fought Military Segregation With ...* https://www.history.com/news/tuskegee-airmen-impact-civil-rights-movement
- *Nancy Grace Augusta Wake* https://www.awm.gov.au/collection/P332
- *Irena Sendler - Wikipedia* https://en.wikipedia.org/wiki/Irena_Sendler
- *Chiune (Sempo) Sugihara - Holocaust Encyclopedia* https://encyclopedia.ushmm.org/content/en/article/chiune-sempo-sugihara
- *The White Rose Opposition Movement | Holocaust Encyclopedia* https://encyclopedia.ushmm.org/content/en/article/white-rose
- *Noor Inayat Khan* https://en.wikipedia.org/wiki/Noor_Inayat_Khan

- *G.I. Joe (pigeon) - Military Wiki - Fandom* https://military-history.fandom.com/wiki/G.I._Joe_(pigeon)
- *Chips (dog)* https://en.wikipedia.org/wiki/Chips_(dog)
- *Antis (dog)* https://en.wikipedia.org/wiki/Antis_(dog)
- *Judy (dog)* https://en.wikipedia.org/wiki/Judy_(dog)
- *Winston Churchill's VE Day Speech In Full* https://www.forces.net/ve-day/winston-churchills-ve-day-speech
- *Hiroshima and Nagasaki: The Long-Term Health Effects* https://k1project.columbia.edu/news/hiroshima-and-nagasaki
- *Brief Overview of Defendants & Verdicts at Nuremberg Trials* https://www.jewishvirtuallibrary.org/brief-overview-of-defendants-and-verdicts-at-nuremberg-trials
- *History of the United Nations* https://www.un.org/en/about-us/history-of-the-un
- *World War II memorials around the globe* https://www.dw.com/en/world-war-ii-memorials-around-the-globe/g-53348668
- *Time of Remembrance and Reconciliation for Those Who ...* https://www.un.org/en/observances/second-world-war-remembrance-days
- *Oral History Resources* https://www.nationalww2museum.org/oral-history-resources
- *During World War II, Literature Reigned Supreme* https://lithub.com/during-world-war-ii-literature-reigned-supreme/
- *Allies of World War II* https://en.wikipedia.org/wiki/Allies_of_World_War_II
- *History of the European Union – 1945-59* https://european-union.europa.eu/principles-countries-history/history-eu/1945-59_en
- *Diplomatic history of World War II* https://en.wikipedia.org/wiki/Diplomatic_history_of_World_War_II
- *Leaders & Shapers - World War II (U.S. ...* https://www.nps.gov/subjects/worldwarii/leadersshapers.htm